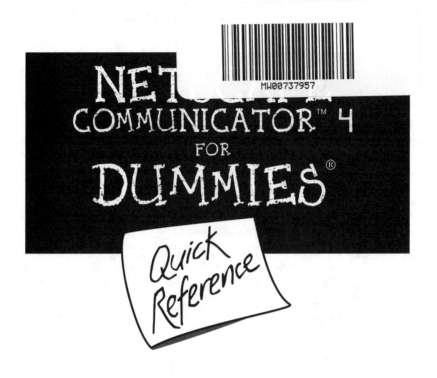

NET[obscured by label] COMMUNICATOR™ 4 FOR DUMMIES®

Quick Reference

by Viraf D. Mohta

IDG BOOKS WORLDWIDE

IDG Books Worldwide, Inc.
An International Data Group Company

Foster City, CA ✦ Chicago, IL ✦ Indianapolis, IN ✦ Southlake, TX

Netscape Communicator™ 4 For Dummies® Quick Reference

Published by
IDG Books Worldwide, Inc.
An International Data Group Company
919 E. Hillsdale Blvd.
Suite 400
Foster City, CA 94404
`www.idgbooks.com` (IDG Books Worldwide Web site)
`www.dummies.com` (Dummies Press Web site)

Library of Congress Catalog Card No.: 96-77276

ISBN: 0-7645-0041-4

Printed in the United States of America

10 9 8 7 6 5 4 3 2

1P/RX/RQ/ZX/IN

Distributed in the United States by IDG Books Worldwide, Inc.

Distributed by Macmillan Canada for Canada; by Transworld Publishers Limited in the United Kingdom; by IDG Norge Books for Norway; by IDG Sweden Books for Sweden; by Woodslane Pty. Ltd. for Australia; by Woodslane Enterprises Ltd. for New Zealand; by Longman Singapore Publishers Ltd. for Singapore, Malaysia, Thailand, and Indonesia; by Simron Pty. Ltd. for South Africa; by Toppan Company Ltd. for Japan; by Distribuidora Cuspide for Argentina; by Livraria Cultura for Brazil; by Ediciencia S.A. for Ecuador; by Addison-Wesley Publishing Company for Korea; by Ediciones ZETA S.C.R. Ltda. for Peru; by WS Computer Publishing Corporation, Inc., for the Philippines; by Unalis Corporation for Taiwan; by Contemporanea de Ediciones for Venezuela; by Computer Book & Magazine Store for Puerto Rico; by Express Computer Distributors for the Caribbean and West Indies. Authorized Sales Agent: Anthony Rudkin Associates for the Middle East and North Africa.

For general information on IDG Books Worldwide's books in the U.S., please call our Consumer Customer Service department at 800-762-2974. For reseller information, including discounts and premium sales, please call our Reseller Customer Service department at 800-434-3422.

For information on where to purchase IDG Books Worldwide's books outside the U.S., please contact our International Sales department at 415-655-3200 or fax 415-655-3295.

For information on foreign language translations, please contact our Foreign & Subsidiary Rights department at 415-655-3021 or fax 415-655-3281.

For sales inquiries and special prices for bulk quantities, please contact our Sales department at 415-655-3200 or write to the address above.

For information on using IDG Books Worldwide's books in the classroom or for ordering examination copies, please contact our Educational Sales department at 800-434-2086 or fax 817-251-8174.

For press review copies, author interviews, or other publicity information, please contact our Public Relations department at 415-655-3000 or fax 415-655-3299.

About the Author

This is Viraf D. Mohta's second book in seven months. He wants nothing more than some time off to return to a normal schedule in which a few hours of sleep are guaranteed each day. Having switched jobs during the writing of this book, he'd like to warn other authors about the pitfalls of a crazy maneuver like that.

His first book was *The World Wide Web For Kids And Parents,* also published by IDG Books Worldwide, Inc. He believes kids and computers make a great combo.

Viraf's 9-to-5 job is at Merrill Lynch in Princeton, NJ. He also acts as technology consultant for other organizations. He holds an MBA in Management Information Systems. He's also an entrepreneur and the 1992 World Champion in Full-Contact Stickfighting. When he finds time, he runs marathons. His goal is to run his next race in under three hours.

He can be reached at `vmohta@hotmail.com`. His Web address is `www.geocities.com/colosseum/2106/`.

ABOUT IDG BOOKS WORLDWIDE

Welcome to the world of IDG Books Worldwide.

IDG Books Worldwide, Inc., is a subsidiary of International Data Group, the world's largest publisher of computer-related information and the leading global provider of information services on information technology. IDG was founded more than 25 years ago and now employs more than 8,500 people worldwide. IDG publishes more than 275 computer publications in over 75 countries (see listing below). More than 60 million people read one or more IDG publications each month.

Launched in 1990, IDG Books Worldwide is today the #1 publisher of best-selling computer books in the United States. We are proud to have received eight awards from the Computer Press Association in recognition of editorial excellence and three from *Computer Currents'* First Annual Readers' Choice Awards. Our best-selling *...For Dummies®* series has more than 30 million copies in print with translations in 30 languages. IDG Books Worldwide, through a joint venture with IDG's Hi-Tech Beijing, became the first U.S. publisher to publish a computer book in the People's Republic of China. In record time, IDG Books Worldwide has become the first choice for millions of readers around the world who want to learn how to better manage their businesses.

Our mission is simple: Every one of our books is designed to bring extra value and skill-building instructions to the reader. Our books are written by experts who understand and care about our readers. The knowledge base of our editorial staff comes from years of experience in publishing, education, and journalism — experience we use to produce books for the '90s. In short, we care about books, so we attract the best people. We devote special attention to details such as audience, interior design, use of icons, and illustrations. And because we use an efficient process of authoring, editing, and desktop publishing our books electronically, we can spend more time ensuring superior content and spend less time on the technicalities of making books.

You can count on our commitment to deliver high-quality books at competitive prices on topics you want to read about. At IDG Books Worldwide, we continue in the IDG tradition of delivering quality for more than 25 years. You'll find no better book on a subject than one from IDG Books Worldwide.

IDG BOOKS WORLDWIDE

John Kilcullen
CEO
IDG Books Worldwide, Inc.

Steven Berkowitz
President and Publisher
IDG Books Worldwide, Inc.

VIII WINNER — *Eighth Annual Computer Press Awards 1992*

IX WINNER — *Ninth Annual Computer Press Awards 1993*

X WINNER — *Tenth Annual Computer Press Awards 1994*

XI WINNER — *Eleventh Annual Computer Press Awards 1995*

IDG Books Worldwide, Inc., is a subsidiary of International Data Group, the world's largest publisher of computer-related information and the leading global provider of information services on information technology. International Data Group publishes over 275 computer publications in over 75 countries. Sixty million people read one or more International Data Group publications each month. International Data Group's publications include: **ARGENTINA:** Buyer's Guide, Computerworld Argentina, PC World Argentina; **AUSTRALIA:** Australian Macworld, Australian PC World, Australian Reseller News, Computerworld, IT Casebook, Network World, Publish, Webmaster; **AUSTRIA:** Computerwelt Osterreich, Networks Austria, PC Tip Austria; **BANGLADESH:** PC World Bangladesh; **BELARUS:** PC World Belarus; **BELGIUM:** Data News; **BRAZIL:** Annuário de Informática, Computerworld, Connections, Macworld, PC Player, PC World, Publish, Reseller News, Supergamepower; **BULGARIA:** Computerworld Bulgaria, Network World Bulgaria, PC & MacWorld Bulgaria; **CANADA:** CIO Canada, Client/Server World, ComputerWorld Canada, InfoWorld Canada, NetworkWorld Canada, WebWorld; **CHILE:** Computerworld Chile, PC World Chile; **COLOMBIA:** Computerworld Colombia, PC World Colombia; **COSTA RICA:** PC World Centro America; **THE CZECH AND SLOVAK REPUBLICS:** Computerworld Czechoslovakia, Macworld Czech Republic, PC World Czechoslovakia; **DENMARK:** Communications World Danmark, Computerworld Danmark, Macworld Danmark, PC World Danmark, Techworld Denmark; **DOMINICAN REPUBLIC:** PC World Republica Dominicana; **ECUADOR:** PC World Ecuador; **EGYPT:** Computerworld Middle East, PC World Middle East; **EL SALVADOR:** PC World Centro America; **FINLAND:** MikroPC, Tietoverkko, Tietoviikko; **FRANCE:** Distributique, Hebdo, Info PC, Le Monde Informatique, Macworld, Reseaux & Telecoms, WebMaster France; **GERMANY:** Computer Partner, Computerwoche, Computerwoche Extra, Computerwoche FOCUS, Global Online, Macwelt, PC Welt; **GREECE:** Amiga Computing, GamePro Greece, Multimedia World; **GUATEMALA:** PC World Centro America; **HONDURAS:** PC World Centro America; **HONG KONG:** Computerworld Hong Kong, PC World Hong Kong, Publish in Asia; **HUNGARY:** ABCD CD-ROM, Computerworld Szamitastechnika, Internetto online Magazine, PC World Hungary, PC-X Magazin Hungary; **ICELAND:** Tolvuheimur PC World Island; **INDIA:** Information Communications World, Information Systems Computerworld, PC World India, Publish in Asia; **INDONESIA:** InfoKomputer PC World, Komputek Computerworld, Publish in Asia; **IRELAND:** ComputerScope, PC Live!; **ISRAEL:** Macworld Israel, People & Computers/Computerworld; **ITALY:** Computerworld Italia, Macworld Italia, Networking Italia, PC World Italia; **JAPAN:** DTP World, Macworld Japan, Nikkei Personal Computing, OS/2 World Japan, SunWorld Japan, Windows NT World, Windows World Japan; **KENYA:** PC World East African; **KOREA:** Hi-Tech Information, Macworld Korea, PC World Korea; **MACEDONIA:** PC World Macedonia; **MALAYSIA:** Computerworld Malaysia, PC World Malaysia, Publish in Asia; **MALTA:** PC World Malta; **MEXICO:** Computerworld Mexico, PC World Mexico; **MYANMAR:** PC World Myanmar; **NETHERLANDS:** Computer! Totaal, LAN Internetworking Magazine, LAN World Buyers Guide, Macworld Netherlands, Net, WebWereld; **NEW ZEALAND:** Absolute Beginners Guide and Plain & Simple Series, Computer Buyer, Computer Industry Directory, Computerworld New Zealand, MTB, Network World, PC World New Zealand; **NICARAGUA:** PC World Centro America; **NORWAY:** Computerworld Norge, CW Rapport, Datamagasinet, Financial Rapport, Kursguide Norge, Macworld Norge, Multimediaworld Norge, PC World Ekspress Norge, PC World Nettverk, PC World Norge, PC World ProduktGuide Norge; **PAKISTAN:** Computerworld Pakistan; **PANAMA:** PC World Panama; **PEOPLE'S REPUBLIC OF CHINA:** China Computer Users, China Computerworld, China InfoWorld, China Telecom World Weekly, Computer & Communication, Electronic Design China, Electronics Today, Electronics Weekly, Game Software, PC World China, Popular Computer Week, Software Weekly, Software World, Telecom World; **PERU:** Computerworld Peru, PC World Profesional Peru, PC World SoHo Peru; **PHILIPPINES:** Click!, Computerworld Philippines, PC World Philippines, Publish in Asia; **POLAND:** Computerworld Poland, Computerworld Special Report Poland, Cyber, Macworld Poland, Networld Poland, PC World Komputer; **PORTUGAL:** Cerebro/PC World, Computerworld/Correio Informático, Dealer World Portugal, Mac*In/PC*In Portugal, Multimedia World; **PUERTO RICO:** PC World Puerto Rico; **ROMANIA:** Computerworld Romania, PC World Romania, Telecom Romania; **RUSSIA:** Computerworld Russia, Mir PK, Publish, Seti; **SINGAPORE:** Computerworld Singapore, PC World Singapore, Publish in Asia; **SLOVENIA:** Monitor; **SOUTH AFRICA:** Computing SA, Network World SA, Software World SA; **SPAIN:** Communicaciones World España, Computerworld España, Dealer World España, Macworld España, PC World España; **SRI LANKA:** Infolink PC World; **SWEDEN:** CAP&Design, Computer Sweden, Corporate Computing Sweden, Internetworld Sweden, it.branschen, Macworld Sweden, MaxiData Sweden, MikroDatorn, Nätverk & Kommunikation, PC World Sweden, PCaktiv, Windows World Sweden; **SWITZERLAND:** Computerworld Schweiz, Macworld Schweiz, PCtip; **TAIWAN:** Computerworld Taiwan, Macworld Taiwan, NEW ViSiON/Publish, PC World Taiwan, Windows World Taiwan; **THAILAND:** Publish in Asia, Thai Computerworld; **TURKEY:** Computerworld Turkiye, Macworld Turkiye, Network World Turkiye, PC World Turkiye; **UKRAINE:** Computerworld Kiev, Multimedia World Ukraine, PC World Ukraine; **UNITED KINGDOM:** Acorn User UK, Amiga Action UK, Amiga Computing UK, Apple Talk UK, Computing, Macworld, Parents and Computers UK, PC Advisor, PC Home, PSX Pro, The WEB; **UNITED STATES:** Cable in the Classroom, CIO Magazine, Computerworld, DOS World, Federal Computer Week, GamePro Magazine, InfoWorld, I-Way, Macworld, Network World, PC Games, PC World, Publish, Video Event, THE WEB Magazine, and WebMaster; online webzines: JavaWorld, NetscapeWorld, and SunWorld Online; **URUGUAY:** InfoWorld Uruguay; **VENEZUELA:** Computerworld Venezuela, PC World Venezuela; and **VIETNAM:** PC World Vietnam.

3/24/97

Dedication

This book is dedicated to Jennifer. You have brought untold happiness into my life. I can't wait to spend the future with you.

Author's Acknowledgments

Many, many months before Netscape Communicator came to market, when it was but a dream at Netscape Corporation, Acquisitions Editor Gareth Hancock offered me the opportunity to write this book. Thank you Gareth.

In the long months which followed, and the ever-changing betas which followed, too, Mary Goodwin who served as Project Editor, never lost sight of our goal. I wish to thank her for tireless efforts and weekends at the office, which ensured that this project stayed on track. It was a pleasure to work with you, Mary. And thanks also for that ever-cheerful voice at the other end of the phone.

Thanks as well go to Suzanne Thomas who served as Copy Editor, and Technical Editor Dennis Cox for his keen eye on the technical details.

The production staff, which toils behind the scenes for every book, rarely comes in contact with the author during the writing of a book. They perform an incredible job in laying out the book just right. Heartfelt thanks to all of you.

I'd especially like to thank Mary Bednarek without whom I would not have been a part of the *...For Dummies* family.

Lastly, I'd like to thank my friend John Mammen for being present on the other side of the Web, always ready to run a few tests, often well past midnight.

Publisher's Acknowledgments

We're proud of this book; please register your comments through our IDG Books Worldwide Online Registration Form located at `http://my2cents.dummies.com`.

Some of the people who helped bring this book to market include the following:

Acquisitions, Development, and Editorial

Project Editor: Mary Goodwin

Acquisitions Editor: Gareth Hancock

Copy Editor: Suzanne Thomas

Technical Editor: Dennis Cox

Editorial Manager: Mary C. Corder

Editorial Assistant: Darren Meiss

Production

Project Coordinator: Cindy L. Phipps

Layout and Graphics: Lou Boudreau, Maridee V. Ennis, Angela F. Hunckler, Todd Klemme, Drew R. Moore, Brent Savage

Proofreaders: Betty Kish, Robert Springer

Indexer: Sherry Massey

General and Administrative

IDG Books Worldwide, Inc.: John Kilcullen, CEO; Steven Berkowitz, President and Publisher

IDG Books Technology Publishing: Brenda McLaughlin, Senior Vice President and Group Publisher

Dummies Technology Press and Dummies Editorial: Diane Graves Steele, Vice President and Associate Publisher; Kristin A. Cocks, Editorial Director; Mary Bednarek, Acquisitions and Product Development Director

Dummies Trade Press: Kathleen A. Welton, Vice President and Publisher; Kevin Thornton, Acquisitions Manager

IDG Books Production for Dummies Press: Beth Jenkins, Production Director; Cindy L. Phipps, Manager of Project Coordination, Production Proofreading, and Indexing; Kathie S. Schutte, Supervisor of Page Layout; Shelley Lea, Supervisor of Graphics and Design; Debbie J. Gates, Production Systems Specialist; Robert Springer, Supervisor of Proofreading; Debbie Stailey, Special Projects Coordinator; Tony Augsburger, Supervisor of Reprints and Bluelines; Leslie Popplewell, Media Archive Coordinator

Dummies Packaging and Book Design: Patti Crane, Packaging Specialist; Lance Kayser, Packaging Assistant; Kavish + Kavish, Cover Design

♦

The publisher would like to give special thanks to Patrick J. McGovern, without whom this book would not have been possible.

♦

Contents at a Glance

Table of Contents

How to Use This Book

I don't remember seeing a manual for Netscape Navigator Version 1.0. Do you? Perhaps because a manual wasn't necessary for a product that was so simple to use. You could do just fine without any help.

Times have changed, and you just may need some sort of reference to get the most out of Netscape Communicator. Communicator bears little if any resemblance to its predecessor, Navigator 3.0. As a matter of fact, the browser in Communicator — Navigator 4.0 — is only one of five components which make up Communicator.

This book gives you the heads-up on this radical product. It shows you the stuff you need to know, without boring you with details. We all have way too many things to do other than worry about the nitty-gritty stuff.

This book shows you how to get things done, via simple and concise instructions. Each of the five components of Communicator — Navigator, Messenger, Collabra, Composer, and Conference — are covered in the book.

Keep this book right next to your family picture on your desk. That way you'll never have to waste precious time looking for it.

About This Book

Netscape Communicator For Dummies Quick Reference does not show you how to use Communicator from the ground up. If you are an absolute beginner to the world of Netscape Communicator, you may want to pick up a copy of *Dummies 101: Netscape Communicator,* by Hy Bender, published by IDG Books Worldwide, Inc., to figure out the basics.

You should think of this book as a quick way to refresh your memory about how to exchange a file using Conference, add a headline to your Web page in Composer, or send your best friend an e-mail. Use this book to get quick answers to your questions so that you can get back to work.

To find just the information you need, use the very complete Table of Contents in the front of the book or the index in the back of the book. Within a part (each part is devoted to a separate component of Communicator), you find topics organized alphabetically.

What Are All These Parts?

This book has been organized into eight parts, each one devoted to a specific component of Communicator.

Part I: Getting to Know Netscape Communicator. This brief part gives you an overview of the various programs that make up Communicator. This is where you also discover how to use the help features offered by Communicator.

Part II: Netscape Navigator Turn here to read about Netscape's latest browser — what's new in it and how to go about surfing the Web with it. Printing, saving, bookmarking, reloading, stopping, finding . . . you find all these topics and more covered in this part.

Part III: Netscape Messenger. This part discusses the e-mail software in Communicator. Here you find instructions for sending, receiving, forwarding, and storing e-mail. Other cool stuff, like maintaining an address book and keeping separate folders for messages, is also covered.

Part IV: Netscape Collabra. In this part, you find out everything you need to know about discussion groups, participating in a newsgroup, following threaded discussions, and sharing information with groups of people.

Part V: Netscape Composer. If you want to create your very own home page, read this part.

Part VI: Netscape Conference. This part describes real-time communication between a group of users via whiteboards, voice-mail, and chat tools.

Part VII: Netscape Calendar. If you want to get organized by keeping an electronic calendar, tracking your tasks, and sending yourself reminders about important duties and dates, read this part.

Part VIII: IBM Host On-Demand. Only nerds need apply to this part about hooking up to a mainframe computer. You know who you are.

You also get a Techie Talk glossary at the end of the book. Bonus.

Conventions Used in This Book

Throughout the book, I ask you to either type commands or choose certain commands from a menu. When I ask you to type a command, my instructions appear like this: type **dir**. In such a case, you should only type the word typed in bold, followed by the Enter key.

When I want you to select an option from the menu at the top of a screen, instead of saying "Click on File and then select Save," I use the following format: Choose File➪Save. The underlined letters in such a command indicate *hotkeys*; you can use hotkeys to activate a command by holding down the Alt key and pressing the underlined letter — in this case F and S.

Cast of Icons

I use a variety of icons to point out essential info that you need to get the most out of Netscape Communicator.

TIP

This icon describes a way to do something in Communicator that you may not have known about otherwise.

WARNING!

Look out! You've just entered the Twilight Zone. If you're not careful, you'll self-destruct.

FAST TRACK

This icon points out items that can help you make your Communicator session faster and more efficient.

NERD ALERT

This is something only a nerd — I mean, a cool, brainy — kind of user may be interested in, which by definition, covers us all.

Part I

Getting to Know Netscape Communicator

Long before you and I started using browsers to cruise the Web, people used groupware to communicate with each other and to get work done at offices and corporations around the world. You may have already heard of software and hardware — but what is groupware, you may be wondering? *Groupware* is a collection of software applications — programs for e-mail, conferencing, word processing, data-sharing, scheduling, and so on — bundled together in one package, each component of which can exchange information with the others without any difficulty.

Netscape Communicator is a great example of groupware. You can use Communicator for e-mail, conferencing, reading newsgroups, and much more. In Part I, I take you through a quick tour of all the programs that make up Communicator, and I talk a little about what makes groupware such a great thing.

In this part . . .

- **Why you need groupware**
- **What each of the programs in Netscape Communicator does**

Introducing Groupware

In a company, you distribute information in a variety of formats, such as spreadsheets, databases, technical documents, e-mail, and memos. Many people in the company may need access to the same information at one time. In order for everyone to use this information effectively, it needs to be easily accessible by anyone, anywhere, regardless of its format or the type of system used to access it. Enter groupware to do just that.

Groupware facilitates a smooth flow of information, including graphics, audio, word-processing documents, spreadsheets, e-mail, and scheduling, among a group of users on a network. Groupware enables the group to collaborate, communicate, and share ideas easily via a common interface. Netscape Communicator, as its name suggests, is just that — a set of applications that lets users share information, interact, and work together on a company intranet, or on the Internet.

Although Communicator is primarily designed to enhance communication within a company, the program works just as effectively on the Internet. And with the help of a really neat service that is built into Communicator, you can find other Communicator users logged on to the Internet, anywhere in the world at any time.

Seeing What All the Components Do

Netscape Communicator (Communicator) comes in two versions — Standard and Professional. The Standard version offers the following programs:

- ✦ Netscape Navigator 4.0
- ✦ Netscape Composer
- ✦ Netscape Messenger
- ✦ Netscape Collabra
- ✦ Netscape Conference

The Professional version offers all the programs included in the Standard version, plus the following:

- ✦ Netscape Calendar
- ✦ IBM Host On-Demand
- ✦ AutoAdmin

Netscape Communicator is available for Windows 3.1, Windows 95, Windows NT, Macintosh, and UNIX systems.

Netscape Navigator 4.0

Netscape Navigator 4.0 (Navigator) is the browser component of Communicator. Navigator allows you to navigate the intranet or the Web, letting you jump from site to site to access the information you need. When you first open up Navigator, you see a window like this:

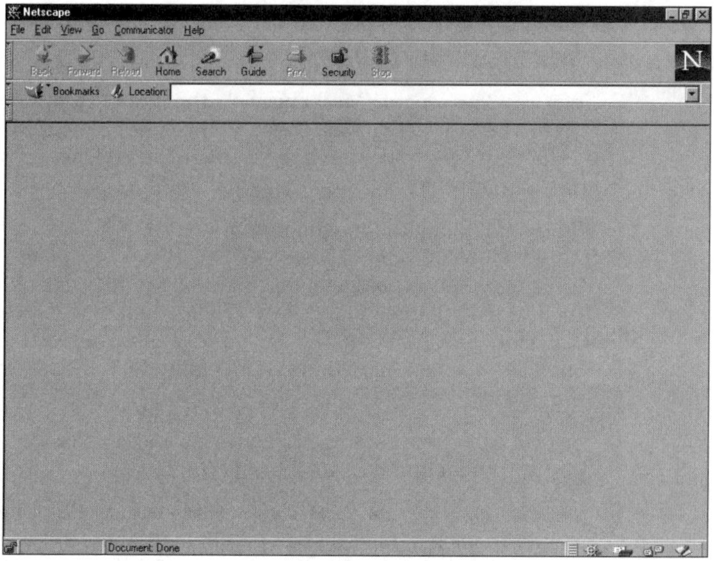

If you used earlier versions of Navigator, you may notice that Version 4.0 bears little resemblance to them. The user interface has undergone a major facelift. Among the many changes, you find a customizable toolbar, the deletion of some buttons from the screen, easier bookmark operations, and drag-and-drop features.

In case you're wondering, *drag-and-drop* lets you perform a certain task by highlighting an icon on the screen and then dragging it, using your mouse, to another location on the screen. For example, if you want to print a document, you can drag the icon representing the document and drop it over the printer icon on the screen. This automatically sends the document to the printer and saves you the extra work of firing up your word processor, opening the document, and then using the menu to print the document.

Drag and drop is only one of the program's many cool features. Some of the others include the following:

✦ You can view and edit Microsoft Office documents, such as Excel spreadsheets, Access databases, and Word documents.

- ✦ Multi-user settings allow your coworkers or family members to retain their preferences, such as personalized bookmarks.
- ✦ You can stop annoying animations from playing continuously on a page you're currently viewing.
- ✦ You can easily go back to a previously viewed page in one action, without repeatedly clicking on the Back button, regardless of how far back you want to go.

Netscape Messenger

Netscape Messenger (Messenger) is the e-mail component for Communicator. Using Messenger, you can write, send, and receive e-mail messages, plus much more, over the Internet or your company intranet.

With e-mail being the most commonly used application on the Internet, careful thought has gone into the development of Messenger. Netscape designed this e-mail component to allow it to do more than just send and receive e-mail messages. Messenger is what Tim "The Toolman" Taylor would call an industrial strength e-mail service. You may find the following features particularly interesting:

- ✦ You can drag links from Web pages and discussion groups and drop them into an e-mail message.
- ✦ You can compose messages in plain text mode or in HTML, which means that you can add images and URLs to a message. (See *HTML For Dummies,* written by Ed Tittel and Steve James and published by IDG Books Worldwide, Inc., in case you need more information about HTML.)
- ✦ A spell-checker saves you the embarrassment of sending messages with errors.
- ✦ You can sort, file, and filter messages based on various criteria.

Just to give you a glimpse of the glorious Messenger screen, here's what you see when you first open the program:

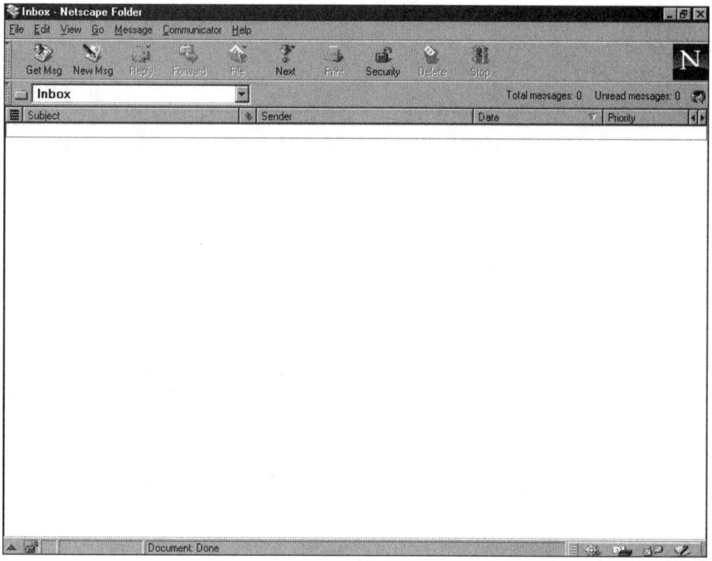

Netscape Collabra

Netscape Collabra (Collabra) allows you to participate in online discussions both on a company intranet and on the Internet. Collabra also lets you efficiently share and track information from these online discussions. Take a look at Collabra:

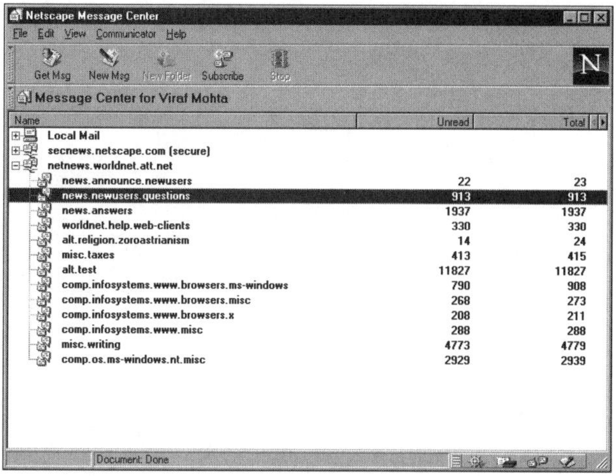

Among the noteworthy features in Collabra are the following:

- ✦ Online discussions take place when one person sends (or *posts*) a message to the forum and other participants read and respond to the message. All responses to a message are listed with the original message, one below the other, in an hierarchial fashion.The messages are *threaded* or linked together, making it easy to follow the discussion. You can even ask Collabra to "watch" and "ignore" certain threads.
- ✦ You can post messages within Collabra in either plain text or in HTML. Hence, you can include images and URLs in messages.
- ✦ You can perform searches for information across many discussion groups or forums at once instead of searching through each forum to find the information you need.
- ✦ You can maintain bookmarks for postings.
- ✦ You can specify expiration dates for postings so that you don't have to look at out-of-date information.
- ✦ Although you may use Collabra primarily on your company intranet, you can also use it just as efficiently for participating in Internet newsgroups, which are also known as *Usenet newsgroups*.

Netscape Composer

Netscape Composer (Composer), as its name suggests, lets you create Web pages and add HTML to e-mail messages and group discussions. This means that you can include *URLs* (Web addresses) and pictures within an e-mail message. Get ready to catch a quick look at Composer:

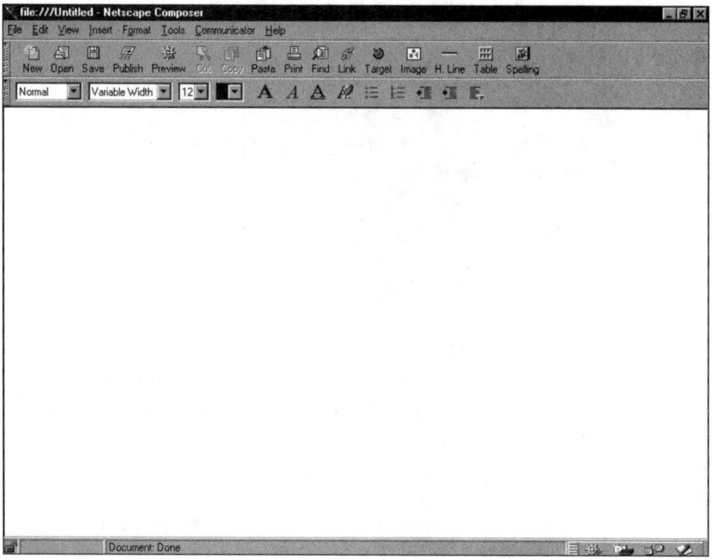

Some of the program's cool features include the following:

- ✦ Composer offers the look and feel of a regular word processor, including features like spell-checking, indenting, font sizes, font colors, paragraph alignment, bullets, and tables.
- ✦ The Page Wizard and Netscape's templates make creating Web pages extremely easy.
- ✦ Because pictures on the Web can be either in JPEG or GIF formats only, composer automatically converts BMP images to these formats.
- ✦ Composer easily uploads documents to the intranet or to an Internet server.

Netscape Conference

Netscape Conference (Conference) is the audio and data collaboration component for Communicator. This component lets users talk with each other as if they were talking on the phone. In fact, using Conference is just about as easy as dialing a phone; for example, when you first open Conference, the program greets you with this nonintimidating window:

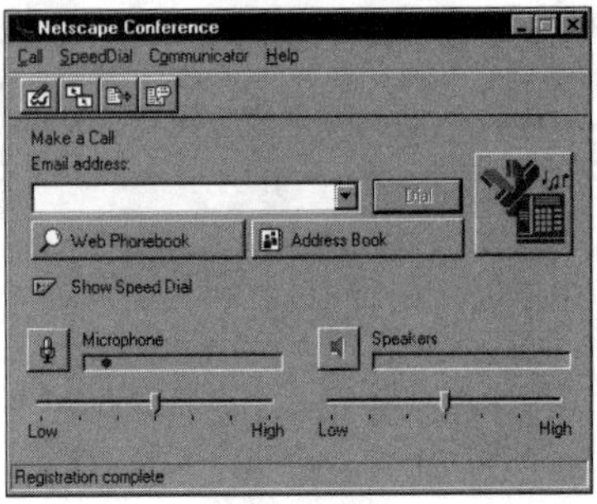

Additionally, Conference offers a chat tool and a whiteboard for text and graphics data conferencing. A *whiteboard* lets several users, each using a separate machine, simultaneously view and edit a graphics or text file.

Conference also offers the following cool features:

- ✦ Full-duplex audio conferencing lets you talk and listen simultaneously, just like a telephone, and unlike a walkie-talkie where only one person speaks at a time.
- ✦ Conference also supports speed-dialing.
- ✦ You can even send voice e-mail from within Conference.
- ✦ Collaborative browsing allows one participant in a conference to lead other participants around the Web. All participants see the same Web page at the same time.
- ✦ The file transfer tool allows conference participants to easily exchange files.

Netscape Calendar

Netscape Calendar (Calendar) is the Communicator scheduling component. It lets you set meetings, coordinate appointments with other users of Calendar, and set reminders about your various commitments. If you use the Standard version of Communicator, you can't experience this great organizational tool — Calendar is only available in the Professional Edition. Here's what the Calendar screen looks like:

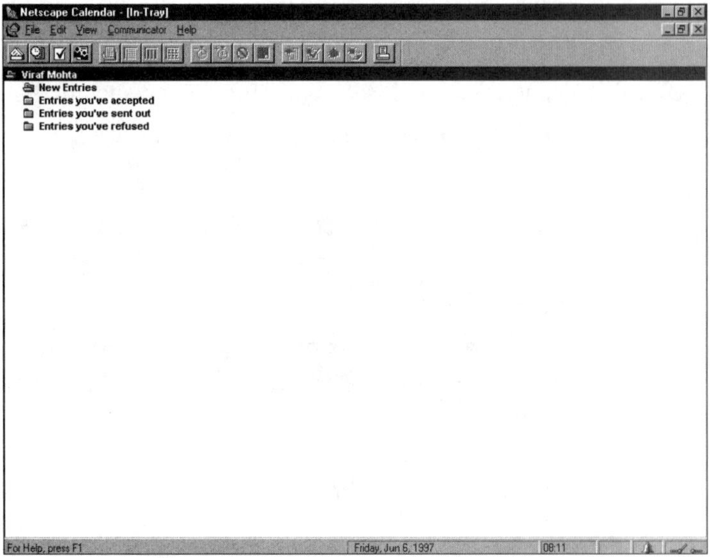

Calendar offers the following features:

- ✦ You can view daily, weekly, or monthly schedules.
- ✦ You can see your schedule in the Franklin, Day-Timer, and Day-Runner formats.
- ✦ You can track tasks and the priorities associated with them, and set reminders.
- ✦ You can assign access privileges for appointments you set in your Calendar to other users. You can either grant full access privileges to such users or grant access on a task-by-task basis only.
- ✦ Calendar notifies participants of scheduled meetings through e-mail.
- ✦ When you go online, Calendar automatically uploads meetings scheduled offline.
- ✦ Calendar adjusts meetings according to your time zone.
- ✦ You can search for available schedules for meetings.

IBM Host On-Demand

Many companies have IBM mainframe computers, which run a variety of software. You usually connect to these mainframes using a *dumb terminal* or using a piece of software called a *3270 Emulator* on your computer. Netscape has included this connection capability in the Professional version of Communicator. This is one nifty feature, because now you don't have to fire up the emulator or use a dumb terminal when you want to use the mainframe computer. You access it from within Communicator.

Those of you lucky enough to need IBM Host On-Demand can look forward to seeing the following when you start up the program:

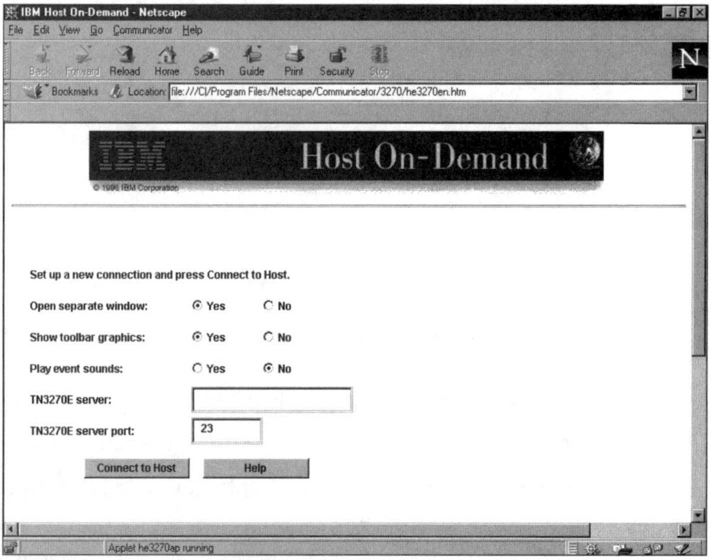

Netscape AutoAdmin

The Professional version of Communicator also offers AutoAdmin. Just think of AutoAdmin as administrative headquarters for Communicator. AutoAdmin makes sure that all users on Communicator within a company use the most current version of the software. Every time you start Communicator, the program checks to see whether you are using the most recent version of Communicator. If you are not using the most recent version, AutoAdmin asks whether the version should be updated. After you request an update, AutoAdmin automatically downloads and installs the upgrade. The program automates and simplifies the distribution, installation, and upgrading process.

Netcaster

Netcaster is a news service. With it, you can get up-to-the-minute news from a variety of sources on the Web. But unlike pointing your browser to a news Web site to read the news, you can have the news automatically flow into your computer without having to go to a specific Web site. That's the primary function of Netcaster — to save you the trouble of going to Web sites for getting your daily news fix.

Although Netcaster is officially a component of Communicator, you won't find it within Communicator. No, it's not an invisible component. It was meant to be included within Communicator, but for one reason or another, Netscape didn't integrate it within the main product. But you can still download it from the Netscape Web site (`www.netscape.com`).

After you arrive at the Netscape site, click on the Get Any Netscape Software link to get to the download section on the Web site. You find Netcaster in the section titled Communicator/ Navigator and Acessories.

The SmartUpdate feature automatically downloads and installs Netcaster within Communicator. After you install Netcaster, you can access the program by choosing Communicator⇨Netcaster within your browser.

A few examples of news sources available within Netcaster are ABC News, CNN, CNNfn, CBS Sportline, Wired Magazine, and Money.com from Money Magazine. Each source is called a *channel,* like the channels on your TV set. After you select the channels you want to get news feeds from, you get current news constantly flowing onto your computer.

Using the Communicator NetHelp Features

Communicator features an extensive set of online help, called NetHelp; each of the components that I describe in this part has a link to NetHelp. To access it, just choose Help⇨Help Contents on the menu bar at the top of the screen or press F1 at any point to bring up the NetHelp - Netscape window.

Topics within NetHelp can be arranged either on a component-by-component basis or as an alphabetical listing of all the contents. You can also perform searches to find help on a specific topic. Here's a look at the NetHelp - Netscape screen, with the topics arranged on a component-by-component basis.

NetHelp - Netscape
Contents
Index
Find
Communicator Overview
Overview
About Navigator
About Messenger
About Collabra
About Composer
About Conference
About Netcaster
About Calendar
About Host On-Demand
About AutoAdmin
Security
User Profiles
Using Help
NETSCAPE COMMUNICATOR
Overview
To display a specific topic, click any item in the left column then click one of the topics that appear below the item. To return to this main contents screen, click the lighthouse (Communicator Help) icon.
These are the main parts of Netscape Communicator; for more detailed information click any of these:
Browsing the Web
Sending and receiving email
Using discussion groups (newsgroups)

To locate information on a particular component:

1. Click once on any of the components listed within the Overview section. This action displays help on various topics within the selected component.
2. Scroll down the list of topics till you find the topic on which you need help.

To find all instances of a particlar word or topic within NetHelp:

1. Click on the Find button. The Find dialog box appears.
2. Type the word for which you want to find help.
3. Click on Find Next. NetHelp finds the first instance of the word you typed and highlights it.
4. To find the next instance of the word you typed, click on Find Next.
5. Click on Cancel after you find the information you need.

To view an alphabetical listing of all topics on which help is available:

1. Click on Index. An alphabetical list of all topics appears.
2. You can either scroll down the list or go directly to a topic by typing the first few letters of the topic name. The list displayed under the Look for box changes to match the letters you type in the Look for box.
3. When the topic you want help on appears in the list, click on it.

To exit from NetHelp:

1. Click on the X button on the toolbar at the bottom of the NetHelp screen. You see a dialog box asking if you want to exit Communicator Help.
2. Click on OK.

Part II

Netscape Navigator

Who said you had to know how to type to use a computer? Navigator disproves that theory. If you can use a mouse, you can see the online world with Navigator. Netscape Navigator is extremely easy to use, and it has an interface that even a child can master within a few minutes.

Version 4.0 is the latest and greatest of Netscape's world famous browser. About 75 percent of all Web users use Navigator to go globetrotting. In addition, because your company intranet works on the same principle as the Internet, you can also use Navigator for browsing your company's intranet.

Navigator 4.0 looks different from its predecessor, and although it works in much the same way, there's a lot more to Navigator than meets the eye. If you've never used Navigator's previous versions, be ready for a treat.

In this part . . .

- **Getting to know some Internet basics**
- **Accessing Web sites**
- **Customizing Navigator**
- **Finding information**
- **Mastering plug-ins**
- **Printing and saving pages**
- **Using bookmarks to get to your favorite sites quickly**

Acquainting Yourself with the Internet

The Internet is nothing more than a bunch — that is a really large bunch — of computers connected to each other. The Internet spans the globe, much like the telephone network. But why the fascination with a really large network of computers, you ask. Well, this network brings the world to your desktop.

After you connect to the Internet, you have access to more information and services than you've ever imagined — from current weather reports to up-to-the-minute stock reports. From baseball scores to movie previews, world news and radio broadcasts, shopping malls and museums, universities and libraries, bookstores and government agencies (including the IRS) — all are accessible on the Internet.

The World Wide Web — or the *Web* as it's affectionately called — is just a part of the Internet. Although the Internet is over a quarter of a century old, the Web is a relatively new thing, born barely seven years ago. The Web differs from other parts of the Internet because of the way in which you can get around it and use the information on it. Getting around the Web requires very little typing, and is mainly accomplished with a point-and-click approach using a mouse.

You navigate the Web through *URLs,* which are addresses that go to *Web sites,* the various locations on the Web that contain those stock reports and baseball scores you need. URLs are the stuff with slashes and *coms* which you see on billboards, newspapers, and TV. In case you've never seen one of these addresses, here's what the URL for CNN, the news network, looks like:

`http://www.cnn.com`

This URL goes to CNN's *Web site* or *Web page* or *home page*. These terms all mean the same thing, although the term Web site is usually used to indicate the main page set up by an individual or company, with links to its other pages.

Armed with a software program called a *browser*, such as Netscape Navigator, you can access a computer or a document on the Internet in any part of the world just by knowing the URL for the computer or the document.

When you get on the Web, you see that some text may appear in a different color or may be underlined. If you move the mouse pointer over this specially formatted text, you'll notice that the cursor arrow changes to a hand with an index finger. This text is not just ordinary text — it's a *link*.

Each link is just a URL to another document or computer. Clicking on a link magically takes you to the document or computer to which that link points, and displays the information contained within the document or computer. The link could point to a paragraph in the same document, to another document on the same computer, or to a document on a computer half a world away.

Accessing a Web Site

When you first fire up Navigator, you need to tell it which Web site you want to go to. If you don't have the Web site bookmarked (see "Using Bookmarks" in this part), you must type in the Web site's URL:

1. Choose File⇨Open Page or press CTRL+O. The Open Page dialog box appears.

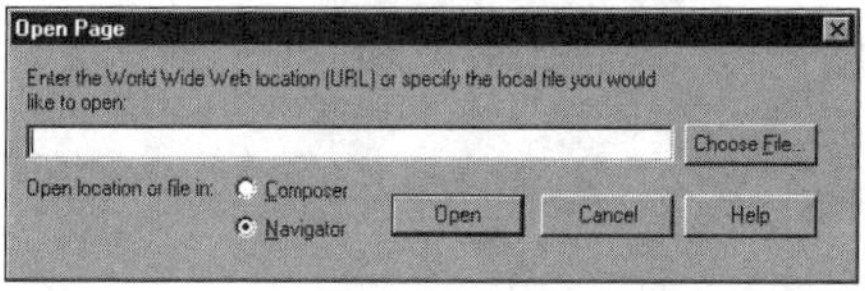

2. Type the URL of the site you wish to visit.
3. Select the Open location or file in Navigator radio button.
4. Click on Open.

Here's another way to do the same thing:

1. Position the cursor in the Location window.
2. Delete the current URL from the window.
3. Type the new URL.
4. Press Enter.

Customizing Navigator

You can customize the Navigator screen to your personal tastes. Don't like the background color of the pages as displayed on your screen? Change it. Don't like the fonts displayed on your screen, either? Change them, too. How about the color of the links? You can customize each of these to your liking as well.

Changing the color or fonts within Navigator on your computer changes the way pages appear on your computer only; you don't permanently modify the contents of the actual page you view.

Changing the background color

Netscape uses gray as the default background color, which you may (understandably) get bored with very quickly. You can change the color of the background by following these steps:

1. Choose Edit⇨Preferences.
2. Click on the + sign next to Appearance to expand it and the choose Colors. The Colors selection screen appears.

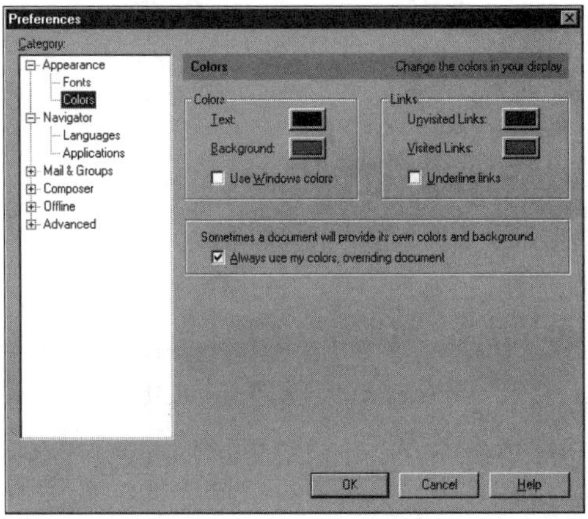

3. Click on the Background color tab. The Color window appears.
4. Choose a color from the palette within the Color window and click on OK.
5. Click on the Always use my colors, overriding document check box.
6. Click on OK.

TIP: Some pages really want you to see the background in a specific color. For example, a page may contain graphics that only look good when viewed with a specific background color. So if the graphics on a particular page look fuzzy, remove the check mark from the Always use my colors, overriding document check box.

Changing the color of text

The default color for text in Navigator is black. How much more boring can things get? To add some spice to how Navigator displays the text on a Web page, follow these steps:

1. Choose Edit⇨Preferences.
2. Click on the + sign next to Appearance to expand it. Choose Colors. The Colors selection screen appears (refer to the preceding figure).
3. Click on the Text color tab.
4. Choose a color from the palette within the Color window and then click on OK.
5. Click on the Always use my colors, overriding document check box.

WARNING! Make sure that the color you select for text is not the same as the background color, or else you won't be able to read anything. That's obvious, you say, but you'll be surprised how many people do this and then wonder what happened.

Changing the font type

Most pages display their text using a proportional font. If the page contains a form in which you can type information, the type of font used for it is usually a fixed font. You can change the proportional and fixed fonts used to the display text on a page. Here's how:

1. Choose Edit⇨Preferences.
2. Click on the + sign next to Appearance to expand it. Choose Fonts. The Fonts selection screen appears.

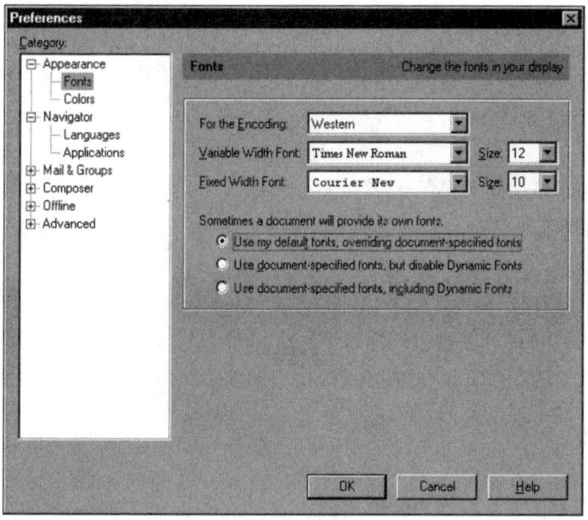

3. Make sure that the For the Encoding box has *Western* selected.
4. In the Variable Width Font and the Fixed Width Font boxes, select the fonts you want Navigator to use. Experiment; try a few different options to see which you like best.
5. In the Size boxes, select the size you want for each type of font.
6. Click on the Use my default fonts, overriding document-specified fonts radio button.
7. Click on OK.

Changing the color of links

Before you go around changing the color of links, you need to know that two kinds of links exist — those you have followed and those you haven't. A blue link tells you that you haven't yet visited it, whereas a purple link indicates that you've been to it.

You can change the color of both kinds of links in the following way:

1. Choose Edit⇨Preferences.
2. Click on the + sign next to Appearance to expand it. Choose Colors. The Colors selection screen appears.
3. Select the type of link you want to change by clicking on either the Unvisited Links color tab or the Visited Links color tab in the Links area.
4. Choose a color from the palette within the Color window and click on OK.

   TIP: Most of the time, links appear underlined. However, if you have to march to the beat of your own drum, you can remove the underline by getting rid of the check mark in front of the Underlined links check box.

5. Click on the check box for Always use my colors, overriding document.

Tracking followed links

You can tell whether you have followed a particular link by the color of the link. The color of visited links is different than the color of unvisited links. But visited links don't retain this different color indefinitely. Visited links retain their color for only 30 days, after which they revert to the color of unvisited links. You can change the time limit for this color change from 30 days to whatever you please. You can even set up Navigator so that it always shows you links you have visited no matter how long ago. Here's how you set these time limits:

1. Choose Edit⇨Preferences⇨Navigator. The Navigator screen appears.

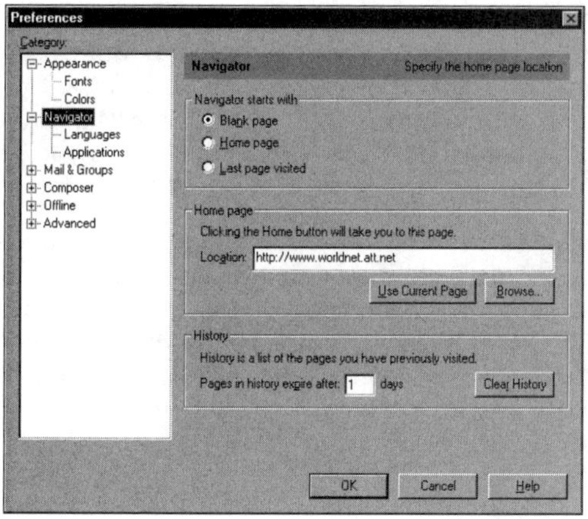

2. In the History section, enter the number of days you want to track visited links in the Pages in history expire after text box.

3. Click on OK.

Starting Navigator with a specific (or no) Web page

Navigator can load a specific page automatically each time you start it. Here's how you set up Navigator to do so:

1. Choose Edit⇨Preferences⇨Navigator. The Navigator screen appears.

2. In the Navigator starts with section, click on the Home page radio button.

   TIP: If you don't want to see any page when you start Navigator, click on the Blank page radio button and then click on OK.

3. In the Location text box of the Home page section, type the URL for the page you want to start with.

4. Click on OK.

Sometimes you may be in such a rush that you don't want this page to appear when you first start up Navigator. Just press the Stop button on the Command toolbar as soon as Navigator starts loading this page and then type the URL of the page you really want to see.

Editing Your Web Page

If you create a Web page of your own, you may want to give it a test run in Navigator. If, after viewing your page, you want to make some changes to it, you can do so right from within Navigator. Communicator ties all its components together, so you can incorporate some of Composer's features into your Navigator session.

As much as you may want to, you can't edit a page that someone else created, no matter how bad the design is. You can't touch the work because the page is on a computer to which you have no editing rights. You can make and store changes only on a computer to which you have editing rights, like your own. If you really can't stand the way a page looks, try changing the color of the background and text (***see also*** "Customizing Navigator" in this part).

To edit your Web page within Navigator, choose File⇨Edit Page. This launches Composer from within Navigator. You can then proceed with your editing. (For a detailed explanation of editing and creating a Web page, ***see also*** Part V.)

Finding Information on the Web

You find more information on the Web than in any library or museum in the world. At last count, 120 million home pages were on the Web. And the number is increasing at an alarming rate. Some of the information is useful — other information, utterly useless. Some information is so useless, you wonder why the author wasted precious time putting it up. But useless or useful, the information is there if you want it, and Navigator provides an easy way to find what you want. Just follow these steps:

1. On the Command toolbar, click on the Search button. The Netscape Net Search window appears.

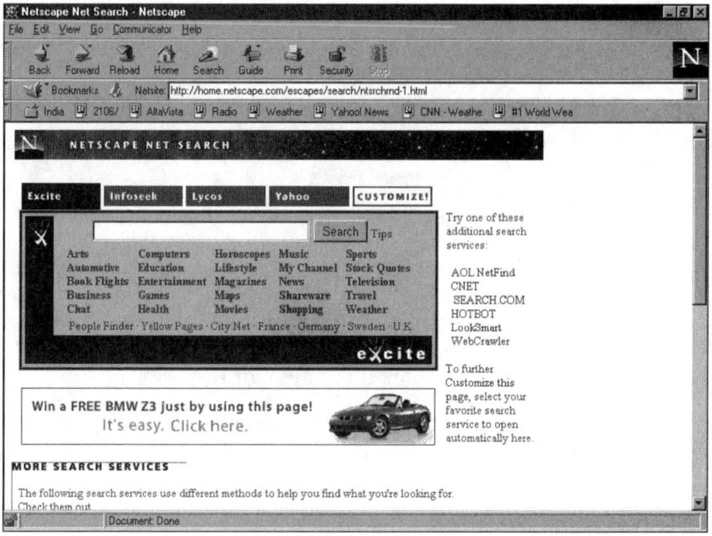

You see buttons called Excite, Infoseek, Lycos, and Yahoo!. Clicking these buttons takes you to *search engines* — software that finds the information you want.

2. To begin a search, click on any of the search engine buttons and then follow the prompts given by the engine you choose.

TIP

If you are not satisfied with the results from a search engine, try another, and another, and another, and. . . . You get the picture.

Finding Information within a Web Page

Sometimes a Web page is so lengthy, it's painful (and slow) to go through screen after screen, looking for the information you want. Navigator makes searching for a word or phrase within a Web page quick and painless, cutting hours off your searching time. Follow these steps to find out just what you want to know on a Web page:

1. Choose Edit⇨Find or press CTRL+F. You see the Find dialog box.

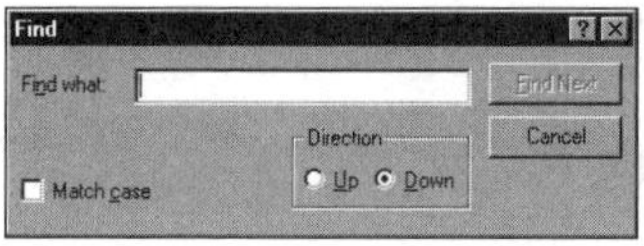

2. Type the word that you're looking for in the Find what text box. Click on the Match case box if you want to find a word exactly as you type it.
3. Click the Up or Down radio button to indicate whether you want to perform the search toward the beginning or the end of the document.
4. Click on OK.

When Navigator finds the word you asked for, it highlights it, but sometimes the word is hidden behind the Find window. You may need to drag the window out of the way to view the word. To continue the search with the same word, click on Find Next. To end the search, click on Cancel, or press ESC.

TIP

Pressing F3 at any time while viewing a Web page executes a search for the last word you looked up.

Plug-ins

A *plug-in* is a special piece of software that works in combination with Navigator to allow you to do all kinds of fun stuff, such as watch video clips, make phone calls, and video-conference over the Web. Netscape has made it possible for software developers to create applications that work seamlessly with Navigator, such as:

- **Shockwave:** A plug-in that allows you to the create and play back fancy animation within a Web page.
- **RealAudio:** Yet another plug-in that lets you listen to live radio while cruising the Web.

Each plug-in has a specific installation or setup procedure that automatically connects it to Navigator. The installation usually takes no more than ten minutes. Once installed within Navigator, the plug-in automatically identifies an application created specifically for it, and automatically plays when the particular application appears on a Web page.

For example, when RealAudio is installed as a plug-in, Navigator automatically plays back live radio when you click on a link within a Web page that connects to a live radio transmission. After the live radio transmission begins, the audio continues to play in the background even if you were to continue to follow links to other Web pages.

Plug-ins are usually available free from the Web sites of companies that create them. For example, the RealAudio plug-in can be obtained from the RealAudio Web site at `www.realaudio.com`.

Usually, if you come across a page that requires a plug-in to view it or use the links on it, you will find a link on the page directing you to the source of the plug-in. Follow the link to the source. You will find instructions for downloading and installing the plug-in. Downloading the plug-in can take anywhere from 5 minutes to 30 minutes or more, depending on the size of the file being downloaded, the speed of your connection, and the type of computer you use.

Printing a Web Page

Navigator can help you find the information you want on the Web. But unless you plan to carry your computer around with you, you may need to print the information you find in order to show it to someone else. Here's how to print a Web page:

1. Choose File⇨Print or click on the Print button on the Command toolbar. The Print dialog box appears.

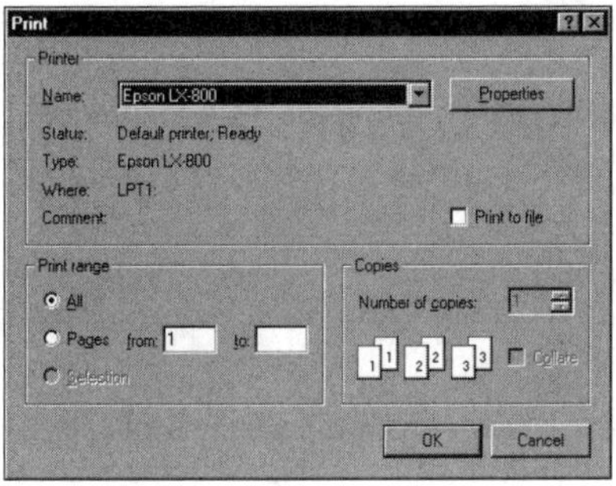

2. If you want to print only specific pages, specify the pages in the Print range section.

3. Click on Properties to specify the paper size and the print quality of the text and graphics.

4. Click on OK.

If you're viewing a page containing frames, the Print Frame option appears as an option in the File menu. This option lets you print only one of the many frames on the page. Position the cursor anywhere within the frame that you want to print and then choose File⇨Print Frame.

To see a preview of the page you want to print, choose File⇨Print Preview.

Reloading a Page

Reloading a page simply means asking Navigator to download the most current information available on the Web page. This is helpful when you're viewing a page that provides rapidly changing information; for example, a page providing running stock quotes. Because the page is constantly updated at its source, you want to make sure that the version of the page you're viewing is the most recent one.

To ask Navigator to go out and get the current version of the page, click on the Reload button on the Command toolbar.

Returning to a Previously Visited Web Page

To return to a Web site that you visited earlier in your Web session, you can do one of the following things:

- ✦ Click on the Back button on the Command toolbar until you get to the Web site. Positioning the mouse pointer on the Back button for a second or two shows you the URL of the Web page you will return to by clicking on that button.
- ✦ Click the right mouse button and choose Back.
- ✦ Press ALT+ ←.
- ✦ Choose Go. In the list that appears, select the Web site you want to go to.
- ✦ Choose Window⇨History. This displays the list of Web sites you have been to. Highlight the Web site you wish to revisit and click on Goto.

Sometimes you may press the Back button once too often in your hurry to get back to a particular page and then realize that you've gone too far back — like when you want to listen to a song one more time on your Walkman. You rewind the cassette for a little too long and then realize that you've gone way past the beginning. What do you do then? You press the Fast Forward button, don't you? The Forward button on the Command tool bar serves the same purpose. You can go forward to a site you've visited in any of the following ways:

- ✦ Press the Forward button on the Command toolbar. Positioning the mouse pointer on the Forward button for a second or two shows you the URL of the Web page you will return to by clicking on that button.
- ✦ Click the right mouse button and choose Forward.

✦ Press the ALT+ →.

✦ Choose Go. From the scroll down window that appears, select the Web site you want to go to.

✦ Choose Window⇨History. Highlight the Web site you wish to revisit and the click on Goto.

Saving an Image on Your Computer

Very rarely will you come across a page that doesn't have a picture or animation on it. Some pictures are cool, others lame. Some are worth saving, others are a waste of time. If you run into a jaw-dropping picture, and would like to save it on your computer, it's as easy as 1-2-3:

1. Move the mouse pointer to the picture and click on the right mouse button.
2. Choose Save Image As.
3. In the Save As window, type a name for the picture and click on Save.

TIP

You can save an animation with a .GIF extension in exactly the same way. Such an animation is just an image file like any other.

Saving a Web Page on Your Computer

You can save a Web page on your computer. Why would you want to do that, you ask. For a couple of reasons.

✦ After a page is saved on your computer, you can view it even if you're not connected to the Internet. This means that when you're cruising the Web and don't have the time to read the entire contents of a really, really long page, you can save it to your hard disk — which usually takes a few seconds — and then view it at your leisure after you have disconnected from the Internet.

✦ If you come across a page that makes you sit up and take notice, you might want to refer to the HTML code behind it for ideas when you're creating your very own page. After the page is saved on your computer you can refer to it whenever you want to. ***See also*** Part V for more information on creating your own Web page.

To save a page to your computer:

1. Wait till the page has finished loading completely. This is usually indicated by the words Document Done on the status bar at the bottom of the screen.
2. Press CTRL+S or choose File⇨Save As.
3. When prompted for a filename in the Save As window, type a more descriptive name than the one that comes up by default on the screen. You'll thank me for this when it's time to look up the file; for some reason, it's hard to remember what is in a file called *chbstr.htm* or *stkht.htm.*

Do not use the following characters in a filename because Communicator uses them to interpret URLs, and the use of these characters could lead to problems:

- slash (/)
- colon (:)
- number (#)

If you're viewing a page that has frames on it, the Save Frame As option is also available on the menu. Use this option to save the current frame.

TIP You can also save a page without displaying it. For example, a page may have links to other pages on it. Instead of clicking on a link, waiting for it to appear, and then saving it, you can save it without having it downloaded and displayed on your screen:

1. Point to the link and click on the right mouse button.
2. Choose Save Link As.
3. In the Save As window, type a name for the file to which you're saving the link and then click on Save.

Sending a URL to a Friend

Sometimes you may come across a page so good that, you'll want to share its URL with the world. You can either type the URL in all its glory — every painful slash, every dot, and *com* — to send it across, or you can do it my way, the easy way:

1. Choose File⇨Send Page.

   Messenger, the Communicator e-mail client, opens a message composing window, where the URL of the current page is automatically typed.

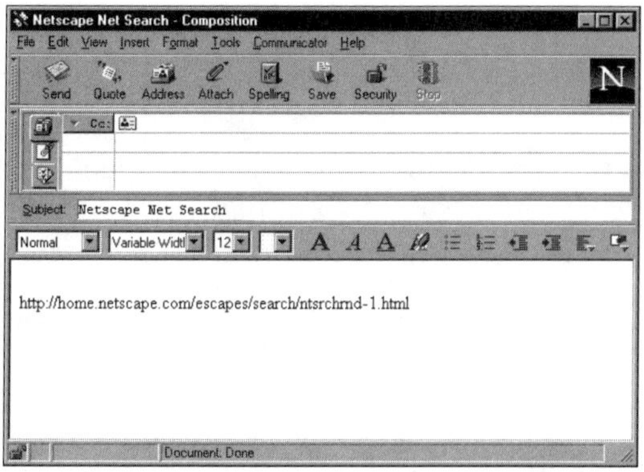

2. In the To box, type the e-mail address to which you want to send the URL.

3. Click on Send.

Toolbars

Navigator gives you three toolbars to enable you to perform common Web-cruising tasks — the Command toolbar, the Location toolbar, and the Personal toolbar.

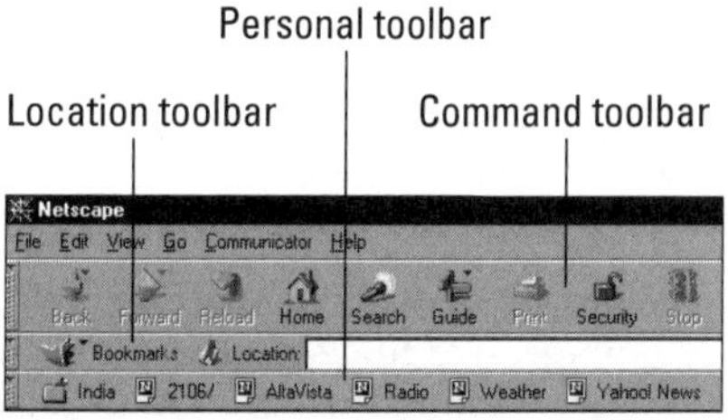

Think of the toolbars collectively as the steering wheel with which you control your journey on the Web. Among other things, you use the toolbars to move around, find information, and print what you see on the screen.

The Command toolbar has the following eight buttons on it:

- **Back:** Lets you return to any Web sites you may have previously visited during your Web session
- **Forward:** Takes you to any available pages in the History listing

✦ **Home:** Displays the Web page you designate as the home page

✦ **Search:** Displays a page containing a collection of search engines

✦ **Guide:** Displays a drop-down menu with options such as The Internet, People, Yellow Pages, What's New, and What's Cool

✦ **Print:** Prints the current page

✦ **Security:** Displays a page dedicated to security related information

✦ **Reload/Stop:** Sometimes the information on a page may not be downloaded to your computer properly the first time. *Reloading* the page downloads the entire page a second time. The description and purpose of this button changes once a page begins to load. It changes to Stop, allowing you to stop the page from loading.

The Location toolbar shows the URL for the page being viewed and also lets you access the Bookmark QuickFile. (***See also*** "Using Bookmarks" in this section for more information on bookmarks.) You can type a Web site's URL directly in the address box of the Location toolbar to go that Web site.

The Personal toolbar is a customizable toolbar on which you can create icons for the URLs you wish to visit often. These URLs can be for Web sites, discussion groups, mail folders, and Address Book entries.

Changing the size of the toolbars

Sometimes you may want to see a little more of the screen and temporarily remove a toolbar from view. To shrink a toolbar, follow these steps:

1. Move the mouse pointer over the granular looking vertical tab to the extreme left of the toolbar that you want to shrink. The pointer changes to a palm.
2. Click. The toolbar disappears, and in its place, you see a granular looking horizontal tab.

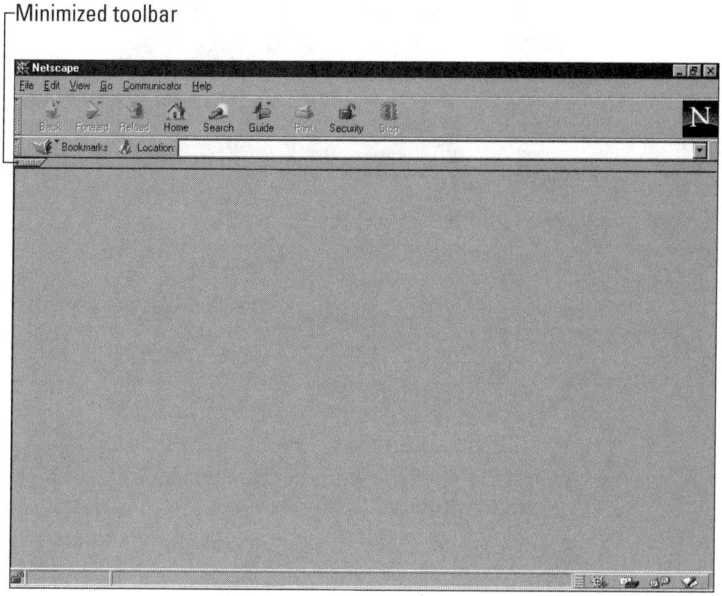

At some point, you may want to use a toolbar that you put out of view. To expand a toolbar:

1. Move the mouse pointer over the granular looking horizontal tab in the top left margin of your screen.

   TIP: If you have more than one toolbar minimized, positioning the mouse pointer over the tabs displays a tooltip balloon indicating the toolbar you're pointing to.

2. Click on the tab of the toolbar that you wish to expand. It should come into full view once again.

Displaying toolbars without text

After you get used to the icons on the Command toolbar and what they stand for, you may want to display them without their names. Here's how you can do that:

1. Choose Edit⇨Preferences⇨Appearance. The Appearance dialog box appears.

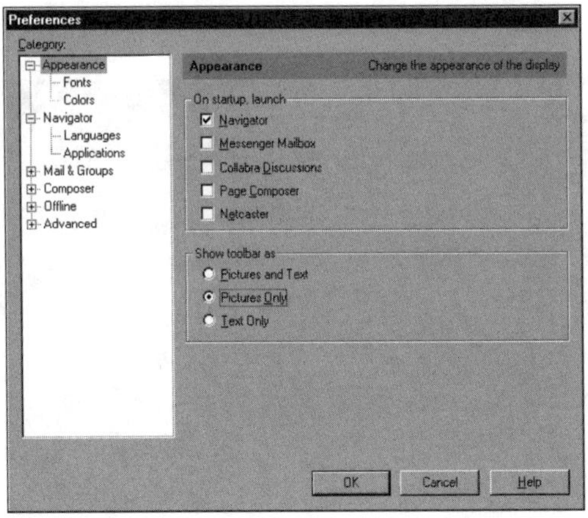

2. In the Show toolbar as section, click on the Pictures Only radio button.

3. Click on OK.

Moving a toolbar

You can move a toolbar above or below the other toolbars by following these steps:

1. Position the mouse pointer on the toolbar.

2. Hold the left mouse button down and drag (in other words, click and drag) the toolbar to the new location.

Hiding (and unhiding) a toolbar

Hiding a toolbar is not the same as minimizing it. When you hide it, you completely remove it from the screen. To hide a toolbar:

1. Choose View⇨Toolbars.

2. Choose the toolbar you want to hide by clicking on it.

To display a hidden toolbar:

1. Choose View⇨Toolbars.

2. Choose the toolbar you want to display by clicking on it.

Uncovering the Component Bar

The Communicator Component bar gives easy access to the browser, the mailbox messages, newsgroups messages, and the composer window via a set of icons. You can set the Component bar to be visible at all times, regardless of the application you're using. This gives you immediate, one-click access to all of Communicator's components.

Displaying the Component bar

You can set the Component bar such that it is visible as a tiny bar at the bottom right corner of the Navigator window.

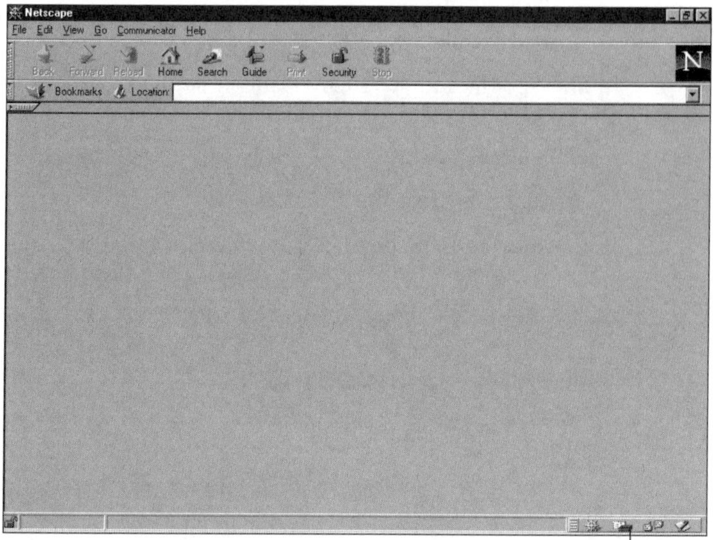

Or you can set it so that it is visible as a separate window that you can move anywhere in the screen.

To put the Component in the corner, choose Communicator⇨Dock Component Bar.

To put the bar in its own window, choose Communicator⇨Show Component Bar. After the bar appears in its own window, you can make that window verticle or horizontal by right-clicking once on the title bar of the Component bar window and then choosing either Horizontal or Vertical.

Uploading Files to an FTP Site

If you've dabbled in the creation of a home page, you know what it's like to create a file and then to upload it to an FTP site or server. If you've never done this, you haven't missed much. Until recently you had to make use of special software to upload files to an Internet server. But now you can do this from within Navigator 4.0. Here's how:

1. Choose File⇨Open Page.
2. Type the URL for the FTP site or server to which you wish to upload the file.
3. Select Browser in the Open location or file in section.
4. Click on Open.
5. Once a connection is established with the FTP site, click on the folder to which you want to upload the file.
6. Choose File⇨Upload File. The File Upload dialog box appears.

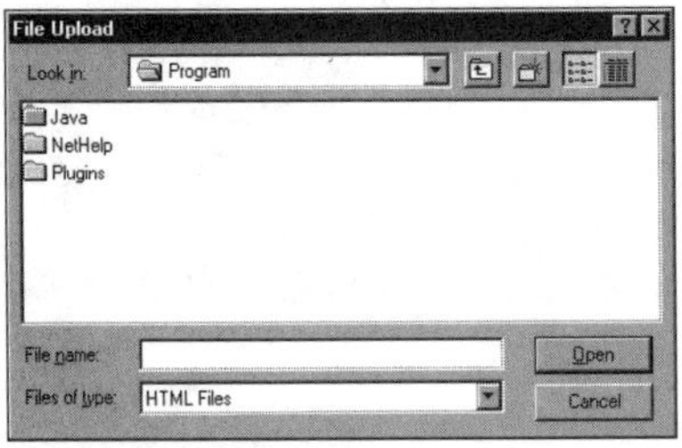

Using Bookmarks

We all know what a bookmark is. It's a little mark you make in a book to help you find a particular page when you need it, fast. A bookmark within Navigator serves the same purpose. When you see a Web site that you think you may want to visit again, you bookmark it. The Bookmark feature is a neat feature, and very helpful, too, because if you cruise the Web as much as I do, you'll come across at least a handful of sites everyday that you'll want to visit again.

Adding a URL to the bookmark list

When you are on a Web site, adding a URL to the bookmark list is extremely easy. You can do so as follows:

1. Position the mouse pointer over the the Page Proxy icon (the yellow icon), which is to the left on the Location toolbar. Notice that the mouse pointer changes to a palm.
2. Hold the left mouse button down and drag the Page Proxy icon over the Bookmark QuickFile icon on the same toolbar. Notice that it changes to a chain-like link.
3. Release the mouse button. The URL for the current page is now added to the bottom of the bookmark list.

Here are other ways to add the URL for the currently displayed page to the bookmark list:

- ✦ Press the right mouse button and choose Add Bookmark.
- ✦ Press CTRL+D.
- ✦ Click on the Bookmark QuickFile icon and choose Add Bookmark.

You can add a URL to a specific folder within your bookmark list as follows:

1. Before you drop the link onto the Bookmark icon, hold the link on that icon for a second. Doing so displays the bookmark list with all its folders.
2. Drag the link over to your folder of choice and then release the button. The bookmark has now been added to the selected folder.

Using a bookmark

To go to a URL listed within your bookmark file, just click on the Bookmark QuickFile icon and then choose the URL you wish to go to from those listed.

To pick a URL bookmarked within a folder, hold the mouse pointer over a folder for a second. This displays the contents of that folder. Then choose your URL.

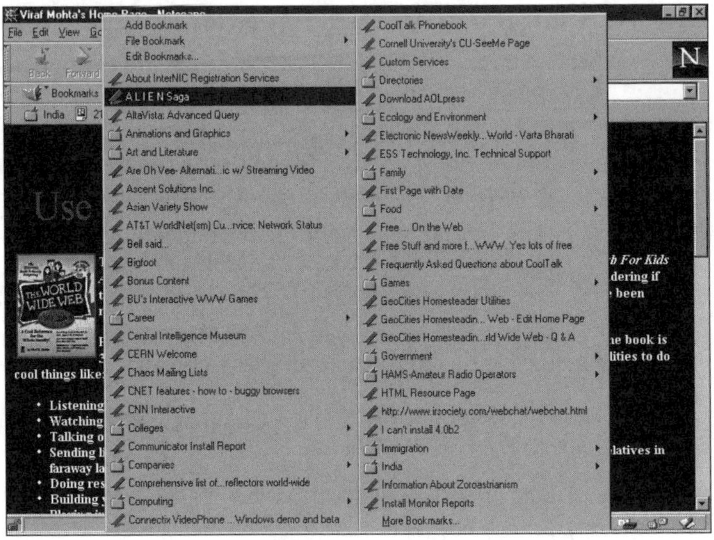

To close the Bookmark QuickFile, click anywhere outside the file or press ESC.

If you don't find your URL either within the list displayed or within the folders displayed:

1. Click on More Bookmarks at the bottom of this list. All the bookmarks you have appear.

2. Scroll down the list till you find the bookmark you're looking for.

3. To exit from the list, choose File➪Close.

Adding (and removing) a URL to your Personal toolbar

The Personal toolbar is one of my favorite features of Navigator. It gives me the freedom to add links or icons as buttons to the toolbar. If I visit a particular Web site at least once a day, I create an icon for it on the Personal toolbar. This way, the site is no more than a click away. Here's how you can add the current Web page to the Personal toolbar:

1. Make sure that your Personal toolbar is displayed and maximized.

2. Position the mouse pointer over the Page Proxy icon (the yellow icon) on the Location toolbar. Notice that the pointer changes to a palm.

3. Hold the left mouse button down and drag the Page Proxy icon to the Personal toolbar. Notice that the icon changes to a chain-like link.

4. Release the mouse button. The URL for the current page appears as an icon on your Personal toolbar.

All links on your Personal toolbar are maintained within a folder called the Toolbar Folder in your bookmark list. To remove a link from your Personal toolbar you must remove it from the Toolbar Folder as follows:

1. Click on the Bookmark QuickFile icon on the Location toolbar.

2. Choose Edit➪Bookmarks.

3. Within the Toolbar Folder, choose the URL you wish to remove from the Personal toolbar.

4. You can either move the URL to another folder, or delete it. To move it to another folder, drag and drop it to the folder of choice. To delete it, press the right mouse button and choose Delete. The bookmark is zapped.

5. Exit from the bookmark list by choosing File➪Close, and check the Personal toolbar to confirm that it no longer contains the link.

Setting (and removing) a Bookmark folder as your Personal toolbar

You can set an entire folder from within your bookmark list as your Personal toolbar. All the URLs within such a folder will appear as icons on the Personal toolbar. Here's how you do it:

1. Open the bookmark file by clicking on the Bookmark QuickFile icon and choosing Edit⇨Bookmarks.
2. Choose the folder you wish to set as your Personal toolbar.
3. Choose Item⇨Set to Toolbar Folder.
4. Choose File⇨Close to exit from the Bookmark list.

The selected folder's bookmarks should now appear as icons on the Personal toolbar.

To clear the Personal toolbar of all icons, assign an empty folder to it. To do so, first create an empty folder:

1. Open the bookmark file by clicking on the Bookmark QuickFile icon and selecting Edit⇨Bookmarks.
2. Choose Item⇨Insert Folder.
3. In the Bookmark Properties window, replace the generic name of the folder (New Folder) with a name that is more descriptive. Because you plan on leaving it empty, I suggest you call it Empty Folder.
4. Choose Item⇨Set to Toolbar Folder.
5. Choose File⇨Close to exit from the Bookmark list.

Sorting bookmarks

Every now and then you'll realize that your bookmark list has become way too lengthy. Finding URLs within becomes a chore. One way to make this easier is to sort the bookmarks alphabetically. Sorting is very easy to do. Here's how:

1. Open the bookmark file by clicking on the Bookmark QuickFile icon and choosing Edit⇨Bookmarks.
2. Choose the very first item at the top of the bookmark list by clicking on it. This item is the root folder in which all other folders exist.
3. Choose Item⇨Sort Bookmarks.

The bookmarks, even those within folders, are now arranged alphabetically.

To sort the contents of a specific folder only, select only that folder instead of selecting the root folder as in the preceding steps.

Creating a new bookmark folder

After a few sessions of cruising the Web, you'll notice that your bookmark file is longer than the tail of Haley's comet (which incidentally could sometimes stretch to about 50 million miles). To organize your bookmarks, I recommend that you store them in folders. To create a folder within the bookmark file:

1. Open the bookmark file by clicking on the Bookmark QuickFile icon and choosing Edit⇨Bookmarks.
2. Choose Item⇨Insert Folder.
3. Replace the generic name New Folder with something more descriptive.
4. Type a description in the Description box.
5. Click on OK.

You should make sure that no two folders have the same name. Navigator doesn't alert you if a folder with the same name already exists within your bookmark list.

Moving URLs between bookmark folders

To move a URL from one folder to another:

1. Open the bookmark file by clicking on the Bookmark QuickFile icon and choosing Edit⇨Bookmarks.
2. Drag and drop the bookmark into your folder of choice.

Using the History File

Navigator maintains a log of the Web sites you visit during a Web session. This log is maintained in the History file and is like a set of footprints you leave behind as you cruise the Web. When you exit Navigator, the program erases the contents of the file, and the log stays empty until you start a new Web session.

At any time during a Web session, you can review the History file and directly jump to a Web site listed there — that is, a Web site you have already been to. To use the History file:

1. Choose Communicator⇨History. You should see a window similar to the one shown in the following figure.

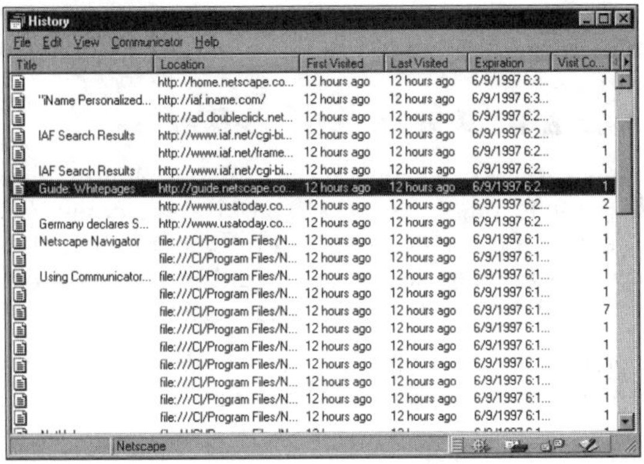

The most recent Web site you visited appears at the very top.

2. Highlight the Web site you wish to revisit and click on Goto.

Part III

Netscape Messenger

Millions of people take advantage of the speed and low cost of Internet e-mail for both their business and personal communications. A disruption in e-mail services for even a day could severely affect a company's operations and touch many people's lives. In fact, e-mail is so popular, it's not at all uncommon for people to have more than one e-mail address.

Netscape Messenger is the e-mail component in Communicator. Yes, you can use Messenger to send and receive e-mail. But Messenger also offers many other cool features that make the program stand out, including an Address Book, rich text capability, and e-mail processing options.

In this part . . .

- **Composing, sending, receiving, and replying to e-mail**
- **Discovering the Address Book**
- **Attaching files to a message**
- **Filtering messages**
- **Using rich text**
- **Managing folders**
- **Looking up people on the Internet**
- **Printing a message**
- **Saving a message**

Acquainting Yourself with Messenger's Toolbar

The Messenger toolbar has a set of buttons that allow you to perform common tasks related to e-mail, such as receiving messages, replying to them, printing them, and saving them. Here's the toolbar with an explanation of its various buttons:

Toolbar Button	*What It Does*
	Checks for new mail and puts it in your Inbox
	Lets you create an e-mail message
	Lets you reply to a message you've received
	Lets you forward a message you've received
	Lets you file a message to a specific folder
	Brings up the next unread message
	Prints a message
	Lets you encrypt a message
	Deletes a message
	Stops a request you've made

Addressing Your E-Mail with the Address Book

The Messenger Address Book is more than just a storehouse for e-mail addresses. It's also a really neat way of maintaining addresses, because it saves you a lot of typing. For example, when you receive e-mail, you can add the sender's e-mail address to the Address Book without typing it in.

In addition to e-mail addresses, you can also maintain relevant information about an individual, including the following:

- Postal address
- Phone number
- Fax number,
- Nickname
- Notes

Although you must type in this additional information, the e-mail address can be added with a couple of clicks of the mouse.

If you send a lot of e-mail to one address, you should consider adding that address to your Address Book. If you only need to send a few e-mails to an address, you can just type the address directly into the To box on the message form.

You can add an e-mail address to the Address Book in two ways. You can automatically transfer the address from a message you receive, or you can manually enter the address. After the address is in the book, though, you can use the Address Book to address your e-mail very quickly and efficiently.

Transferring an address from a message

If you hate typing e-mail addresses, then you're in luck. With Messenger, all you have to do is wait until someone sends you an e-mail, and then you can shuffle the address straight into your Address Book without typing so much as one letter.

To transfer an address to the Address Book, follow these steps:

1. Open a message you receive by double-clicking on it in the Message List window. You see the contents of the message.
2. Choose Message⇨Add to Address Book. A menu appears offering the following two options:
   - **Sender:** Adds only the sender of the message to the Address Book.
   - **All:** Adds all recipients of the message to the Address Book.

3. Choose either Sender or All.

Don't look now, but the address is now safely stored in your Address Book. How difficult was that? Not very.

Typing an address in the Address Book

To type an address in the Address Book, follow these steps:

1. Choose Communicator⇨Address Book. The Address Book dialog box appears.
2. Click on New Card. The New Card dialog box appears.
3. In the New Card dialog box, fill in the relevant information about the individual.

   TIP: You can use a nickname on the To line of a message in place of the lengthy e-mail address it may represent. You can just type the nickname, which is always easier to remember, and leave the nickname-to-e-mail address conversion up to Messenger — the program's pretty good at that.

   WARNING! If the person you just added to the Address Book doesn't have the capability to receive e-mail in rich text format, make sure that you remove the check mark from the Prefers to receive HTML check box.

   If you'd like to add additional information about the person whose information you're entering, then click on the Contact tab. The Contact dialog box appears in which you can continue adding other relevant information about the individual. With this information in place, you can use the Address Book like a Rolodex to store more than just e-mail addresses.
4. Click on OK.

Any e-mail addresses in the Address Book appear with an icon next to them. The following figure shows the Address Book window with an address listed. Notice the icon to the left of the individual's name. It's the e-mail address icon.

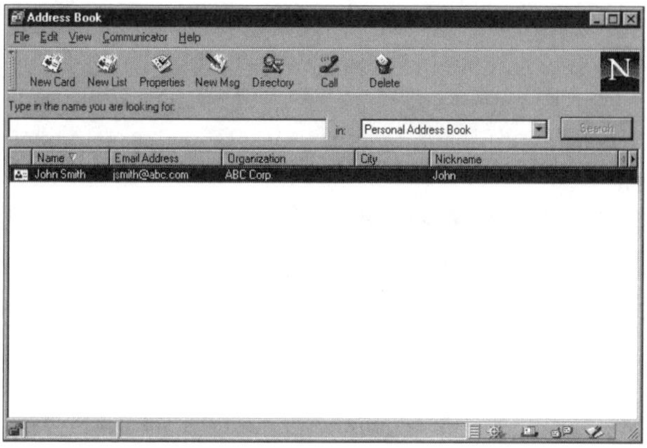

Mailing lists, ***see also*** "Creating an e-mail address list" in this part, appear with a different icon so that you can easily tell the two types of addresses apart.

Editing an address in the Address Book

To change an address in the Address Book:

1. Choose Communicator⇨Address Book to open the Address Book.
2. Double-click on the entry you want to edit, or highlight it and click on Properties. The Card for dialog box appears, containing information about the address you selected.
3. Make changes to the information.
4. Click on OK after you're done making your changes.

Creating an e-mail address list

You may regularly find yourself sending out the same message to several people. Instead of sending the message to each person individually, you can send the message to all of them in one step. You do this by first creating a *mailing list,* which is a list containing the e-mail addresses of all the people you want to send the message to. You give the list a name and then use that name in the To box in your message.

Messenger then does the rest of the work for you by sending the message individually to every person on the list.

Here's how you create a mailing list or an e-mail address list:

1. Choose Communicator⇨Address Book to open the Address Book window.
2. Click on New List. The Mailing List dialog box appears.

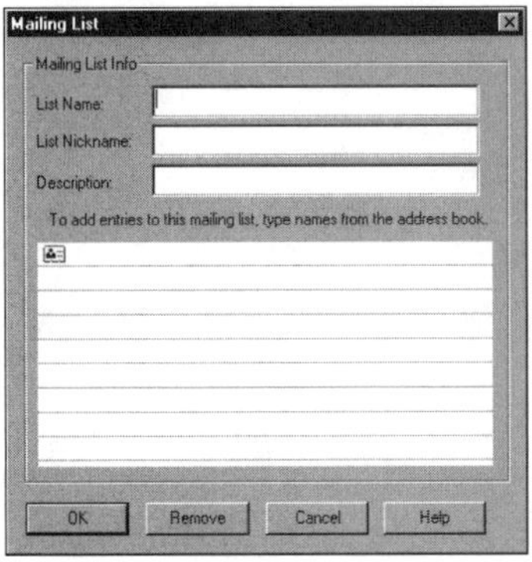

3. Type a name, nickname, and description for the list.
4. Move the cursor to the first line in the address entry portion of the dialog box, type the e-mail address of an individual, and press Enter. Type in the addresses of all the people you want to receive the message, typing one e-mail address per line.

   If the person you're adding to the mailing list is listed in your Address Book, as you begin typing the names of the individuals, the remainder of the name automatically appears on the line in gray letters. If the name which appears on the line is the name you were typing, just press Enter. Messenger finishes up the dirty work by typing up the entire name and e-mail address for you.
5. After you enter the last e-mail address, click on OK.

   If any of the addresses in the mailing list are not already in the Address Book, you see a prompt asking you if you wish to add the address to the Address Book. Click on OK, because the address can be on the mailing list only if it is within the Address Book, too. Communicator automatically adds the address to the Address Book. Your Mailing List is finished and ready to use.

A mailing list entry in the Address Book is distinguishable from a single e-mail address entry by the icon next to it. A single e-mail entry appears with this icon:

A mailing list entry has this icon next to it:

Addressing your e-mail

When it comes time to address your e-mail, save time by using the addresses and mailing list groupings in your Address Book. Using an address or mailing list from your Address Book is as easy as pointing your mouse and clicking it:

1. Click on New Msg on the Messenger toolbar to bring up the Composition screen.
2. If you know that the recipient of your message is listed in your Address Book, just type the first few letters of the recipient's name in the To box. Messenger suggests the remainder of the name by typing it in gray letters. If the suggested name is the name of the recipient, press Enter. If you'd rather select a name directly from the Address Book, click on the Address button on the toolbar to open the Select Addresses window.

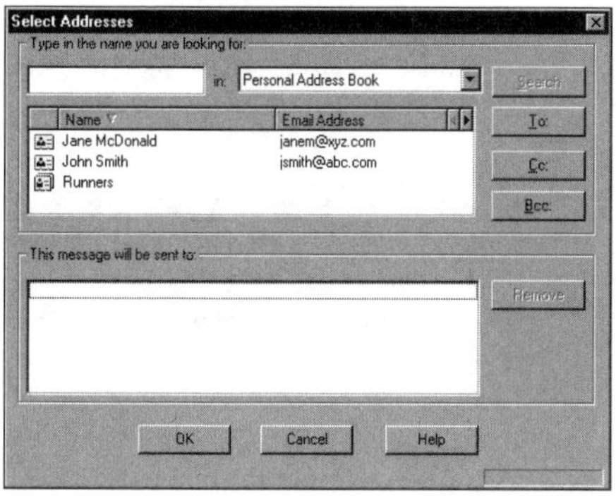

3. Tell Messenger to whom you want to send the message.

   If you see the address you want in the Address window, select it by clicking on the address and then clicking on To. The address should appear in the This message will be sent to window.

   If the address you're looking for is not visible, you can look it up in the Address Book. Type the name of the person you're looking for in the search window at the top of the Select Addresses window. As you start typing, you notice that the names in the Address window automatically scroll to match the letters you type in the search window. When you find the address you're looking for, select it by clicking on To. You can add more than one address to the To line.

Cc stands for carbon copy. Click the Cc: button to send a copy of the message to someone else.

Bcc stands for blind carbon copy. If you want to send a copy of your message to a person without the other recipients knowing about it, you can send a blind carbon copy. Just click the Bcc: button and fill in the address of the person you want to send the blind copy to.

FAST TRACK

If you know that the recipient of your message is listed in your Address Book, just type the first few letters of the recipient's name in the To box. Messenger suggests the remainder of the name by typing it in gray letters on the To line. If the suggested name is the name of the recipient, press Enter.

Attaching a File to a Message

Sending plain text e-mail messages can get boring after a while. Thank goodness that Communicator livens things up by allowing you to send pictures, word-processing files, Web pages, and other files attached to your messages. You can even attach more than one file to a message.

TIP

Although you can attach as many files as you want to a message, you should remember that the larger the number or size of attachments, the longer the message takes to get to your recipient. Also, some e-mail services and e-mail software have limitations on the size of the attachments that you can send. Check with the recipient about such limitations before sending a file. If possible, use compression software (like PKZip or WinZip) to compress files and package several files into a single file prior to sending them. Compressing files makes them smaller and, thereby, faster to send.

Here's how you attach a file to a message:

1. Click on New Msg on the Messenger toolbar to begin composing a message.
2. Fill in the relevant information, such as the address of the person you're sending the message to and the text of the message. Also, notice that the color of the paper clip to the left of the address window is blue.
3. Click on Attach on the Messenger toolbar. The drop-down menu displays the attachment options.

   Click on File to attach a word-processing document, spreadsheet, or picture to your e-mail message. The Enter file to attach window appears. Select the file you want to attach, and click on OK.

Click on Web Page to attach a Web page. Specify the URL of the Web page in the Please Specify the Location to Attach window. Click on OK.

When you attach a Web page to a message, the recipient sees the actual Web page in the body of the message, complete with images and links, if the page has any. The Web page appears as if you had copied it in its entirety into the message.

The name of the attached file or the URL of the attached Web page appears on the Attach Files and Documents tab in the Composition window. Notice that the color of the paper clip on the attachment tab has changed from blue to red, an indication that a document has been attached to the message.

If you attach more than one file, all the attached files appear listed one above the other in the Attach Files and Documents tab in the Composition window.

WARNING! If you accidentally attach a file twice, Messenger doesn't alert you of this error. Make sure that you check the file listing before you send the message on its way.

Checking for New Mail

Messenger automatically alerts you when new messages have arrived. The Messenger icon in the Component bar changes to include a downward-pointing green arrow:

You have a new message.

If you see that green arrow next to the Messenger icon in the Component bar, you have messages to download and read. ***See also*** "Reading E-Mail" in this part for tips on reading your new messages.

Composing and Sending a Message

When you feel you have to get the word out, take a few moments to think about what you want to say, make sure that you're connected to the Internet or your company network, and then follow these steps to write and send your message:

1. Click on New Msg on the Messenger toolbar, press CTRL+M, or choose Message⇨New Message. The Composition window appears.

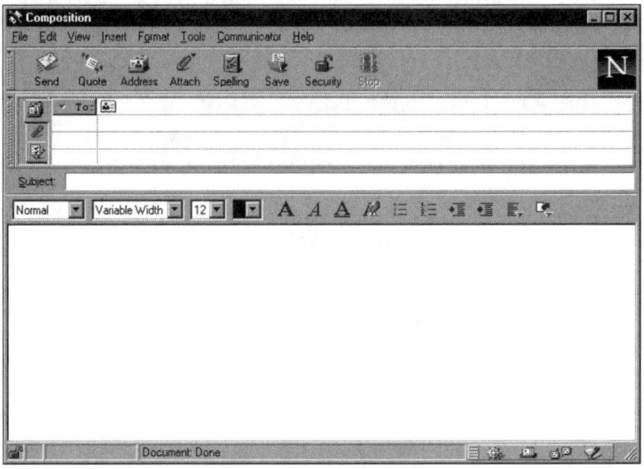

2. Type the e-mail address of the person you're sending the message to in the To line. ***See also*** the "Addressing your e-mail" section for information on how to add one or more e-mail addresses to your message.
3. Type a brief description of the message in the Subject line to give your reader some indication of what your message is about (and consequently whether they want to read the message or not).
4. Type the text of the message in the Message Composition area.
5. Click on Send.

Drafting a Message

At times, you may sit down to compose a message, get halfway through it, and get interrupted to attend to something else. Don't you just hate that? Rather than send an incomplete message, or close the message and then start all over again later, you can save the message as a draft. You can then edit the draft at any time. Here's how you create a draft:

1. Click on New Msg in the Messenger toolbar to begin creating a message.
2. Begin writing your message.

3. Click on Save.

   This saves the message in the Drafts folder, but leaves the Composition window open.

4. Close the Composition window by clicking on the Close icon (the X) in the upper-right corner of the title bar.

Okay, so you got halfway through a message, saved it as a draft, and now want to continue where you left off. Here's how you do that:

1. Click on the Message Center icon and double-click on Drafts within the folder that appears. All the messages within the Drafts folder appear.

2. Double-click on the message you want to work on to select it. This opens the message within the Composition window. You can now continue where you left off.

Encrypting Your E-Mail

Everyone agrees that there's nothing worse than a snoop, whether it's your coworker, your spouse, or your mother. *Encrypting* your messages lets you stop these would-be know-it-alls dead in their tracks. Encrypting scrambles the contents of your messages to make them unreadable without proper authorization.

Encryption within Messenger is made possible by the use of *digital certificates.* A digital certificate is an electronic ID which is unique to you. To use encryption within Messenger, the sender and recipient both need to have unique digital certificates.

Netscape doesn't issue digital certificates, but you can get them from a variety of companies which are in the business of electronic security. Although you need to pay an annual fee for a digital certificate, you can often try one for free for a period of six months.

Acquiring a digital signature

You can acquire a free trial digital certificate by following these steps:

1. Click on the Security button on the Messenger toolbar. The Security Info window appears.

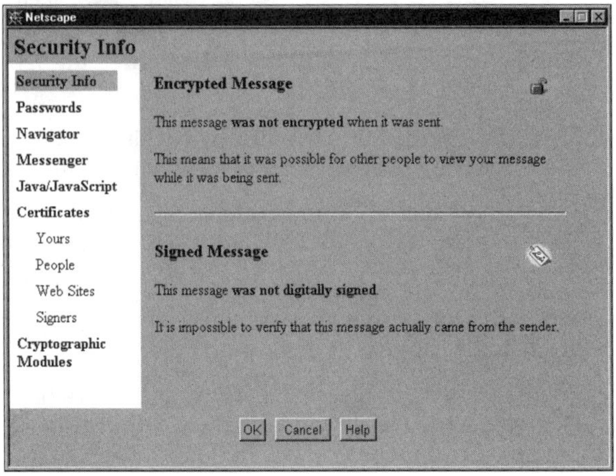
Netscape
Security Info
Security Info
Passwords
Navigator
Messenger
Java/JavaScript
Certificates
Yours
People
Web Sites
Signers
Cryptographic Modules
Encrypted Message
This message was not encrypted when it was sent.
This means that it was possible for other people to view your message while it was being sent.
Signed Message
This message was not digitally signed.
It is impossible to verify that this message actually came from the sender.
OK
Cancel
Help

2. Just for the heck of it, look to see if you have a certificate already (your Systems Administrator may have provided you with one without your knowledge). In the Security Info window, click on Yours, which you find under the Certificates title in the left column. The Your Certificates window appears. If you had any digital certificates, you would find them here.

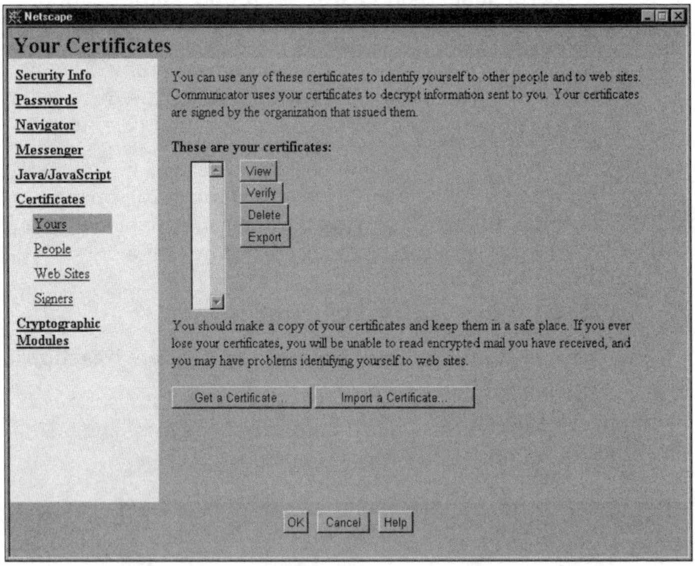
Netscape
Your Certificates
Security Info
Passwords
Navigator
Messenger
Java/JavaScript
Certificates
Yours
People
Web Sites
Signers
Cryptographic Modules
You can use any of these certificates to identify yourself to other people and to web sites. Communicator uses your certificates to decrypt information sent to you. Your certificates are signed by the organization that issued them.
These are your certificates:
View
Verify
Delete
Export
You should make a copy of your certificates and keep them in a safe place. If you ever lose your certificates, you will be unable to read encrypted mail you have received, and you may have problems identifying yourself to web sites.
Get a Certificate...
Import a Certificate...
OK
Cancel
Help

3. Scroll down the window and click on Get a Certificate. Messenger takes you off to the Certificates Authority Services page

on the Netscape Web site, where you see several links for providers of digital authentication products and services.

4. Click on VeriSign, which takes you to the VeriSign Web site. VeriSign provides a free digital certificate to anyone for a test period of six months.
5. Click on Product Overview. The Product Overview page appears, listing VeriSign's various products and services.
6. Click on Individuals.
7. Click on Digital ID Test Drive. The Digital ID Test Drive page appears.
8. Scroll down the page and click on Go to the ID Center.
9. At the ID Center, click on Request an ID, and follow the instructions to get a digital certificate.

After you sign up for a digital certificate with either VeriSign or some other vendor, check to see that your certificate is up and running by clicking on the Security button in the Messenger toolbar. You should see your digital certificate listed in the Security Info window.

TIP

You can obtain digital certificates from as many vendors as you want.

Getting encrypted messages

Your digital certificate contains your digital signature, a code which identifies you. When you send an e-mail message and add your digital signature to it, you include your digital certificate within your message, which gives the recipient of your message the ability to send an encrypted reply to you.

Your digital certificate automatically gets added to the list of valid digital certificates on your recipient's computer. The next time the recipient wants to send an encrypted message to you, your digital certificate encrypts the message to you.

Similarly, when you receive a digitally signed message from someone, Messenger automatically adds the sender's digital certificate to your computer. To see the list of people for whom you have digital certificates, follow these steps:

1. Click on the Security button on the Messenger toolbar. The Security Info window appears.
2. Click on People under the Certificates heading in the left column. You see a list of people from whom you have received digital certificates.

Exporting and importing digital certificates

A digital certificate is only usable on the computer on which it was obtained. To use it on another computer, the digital signature must be exported from the computer on which it was obtained and then imported to the computer on which it is to be used.

To export a digital certificate:

1. Click on the Security button on the Messenger toolbar. The Security Info window appears.
2. Click on Yours under the Certificates heading in the left column. A list of all your digital certificates appears.
3. Select the certificate you want to export.
4. Click on Export. The File to Export window appears.
5. Save the file on a floppy disk so that you can import it to another computer.

To import a digital certificate:

1. Click on the Security button on the Messenger toolbar. The Security Info window appears.
2. Click on Yours under the Certificates heading in the left column. A list of all your digital certificates appears.
3. Scroll down the window until you see the Import a Certificate button.
4. Click on the Import a Certificate button. The File Name to Import dialog box appears.
5. Select the file to import.

Messenger automatically imports the digital certificate, saves it, and lists it with your other digital certificates.

Distributing your digital certificate

If you wish to receive encrypted e-mail from someone, the sender must have a copy of your digital certificate. You can give that person your digital certificate by sending a message digitally signed by you. To send a digitally signed message:

1. Click on New Msg on the Messenger toolbar. The Composition window appears.
2. Click on the Security button on the Messenger toolbar. The Security Info window appears.
3. Scroll down the window to the Signing Message section.

4. Click on the check box for Include my Security Certificate in this message and use a digital signature to sign this message. A check mark should appear in the box.
5. Click on OK. You return to the Composition window. Notice that the lock on the Security button now has a tag on it.
6. Type the recipient's address in the To box.
7. Click on Send.

When the recipient reads your message, your digital certificate will automatically be added to the list of digital certificates on the recipient's computer. Now the recipient can send encrypted messages to you.

Sending an encrypted message

You need to have a digital certificate to be able to send an encrypted message. ***See also*** "Acquiring a digital signature" in this part for instructions on obtaining a digital certificate.

The recipient of your message needs to have a digital certificate as well, and should have distributed a valid digital certificate to you. ***See also*** "Distributing your digital certificate" for instructions on distributing digital certificates.

To send an encrypted message:

1. Click on the New Msg button on the Messenger toolbar. The Composition window appears.
2. Compose your message.
3. Type the name of the recipient in the To box.
4. Type the subject of the message in the Subject box.
5. Click on the Security button on the Messenger toolbar. The Security Info window appears.
6. Click on the Encrypt message box. The box should now have a check mark in it.
7. Click on the check box for Include my Security Certificate in this message and use a digital signature to sign this message. You should now see a check mark in the box.
8. Click on OK. You return to the Composition window.
9. Click on Send.

Messenger encrypts your message and sends it on its way.

Reading an encrypted message

Reading an encrypted message is just like reading any other message. Just click on the message header in the Messenger window. Messenger automatically decrypts the message and displays its contents.

Filtering Messages with Rules

Rules, a very powerful feature that, until recently, was available only in high-end, fancy e-mail packages, makes managing your e-mail a snap. Netscape's decision to add rules to Messenger makes Messenger a worthy alternative to most e-mail packages used today.

Rules are essentially a set of instructions for automatically processing and filtering mail messages. This feature can really lessen your workload. For example, say you want to file all messages from your mother, who now floods you with e-mails because your answering machine is on the blink, in a folder called GoodOleMom. You can either file each of Mom's messages in that folder manually every time you receive one, or you can set up a rule in Messenger that automatically dumps, I mean *files*, Mom's messages in the folder the moment they arrive.

You can filter your messages with many different types of rules, but outlining all these different ways of using rules is way beyond the scope of this book. Here, I show you how to filter messages from one source (either a person or mailing list) into one place (a special folder you create just for the purpose):

1. Choose Edit⇨Mail Filters. You see the Mail Filters dialog box.

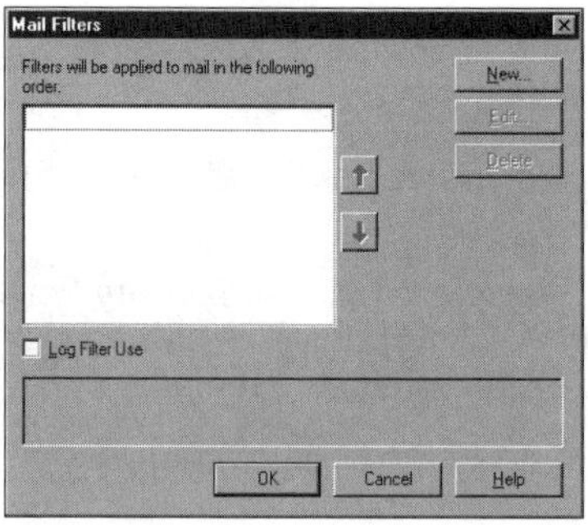

2. Click on New. The Filter Rules dialog box appears.

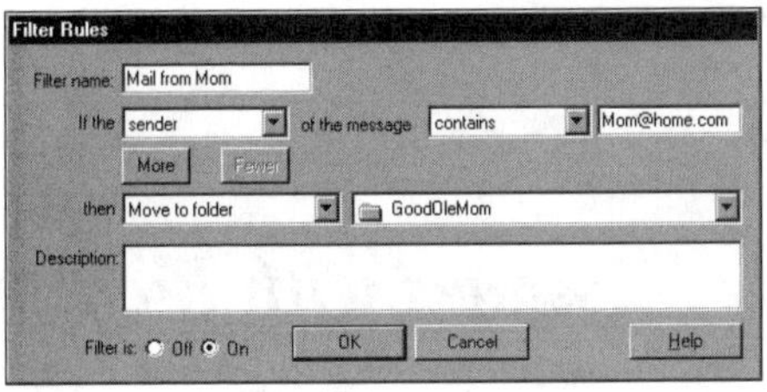

3. Replace *Untitled* in the Filter name box with something more meaningful.

4. In the next line of the dialog box, make sure that the boxes read "If the sender of the message contains."

5. After the box that reads "contains" type the e-mail address of the source of the e-mail you wish to filter.

6. In the next line of the form, make sure that the box next to "then" reads "Move to folder."

7. Tell Messenger where you want it to store your e-mail.

   If you have already created a folder, just use the arrow next to the box to tell Messenger where the folder is located.

   To create a folder, choose File⇨New Folder. The New Folder window appears. Type the name of the folder that you're creating in the Name box. Click on OK.

   If you get adventurous, you can add more criteria to your rule by clicking on the More button.

   The following figure shows what the rule would look like if you decided to filter messages from Mom that contained recipes into a folder called Mom's Recipes.

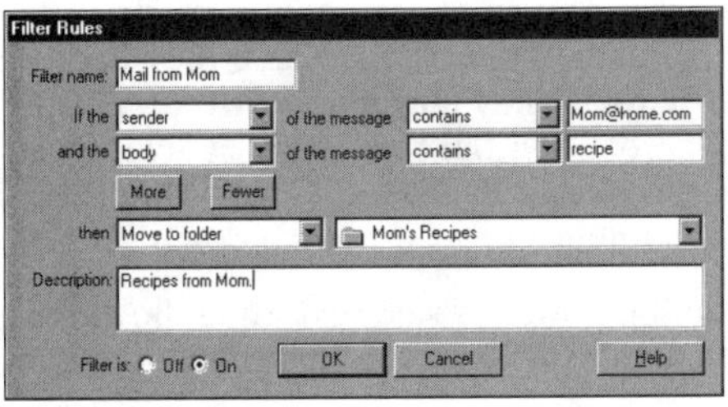

8. Add a description for the rule in the Description box. This description will help you understand what the rule is for when you open it a few months from now.

9. Make sure that the Filter is radio button at the bottom of the window is set to On.

10. Click on OK.

Formatting Your Messages with Rich Text

Plain text, also called *ASCII text* by computer nerds, is very functional, but boring. With plain text, you can't bold, underline, or italicize any of the text in your message. A message composed in plain text is just that — plain.

Until recently, if you wanted to emphasize something in your e-mail messages, you used capital letters. Not any more — at least, not if you're using Messenger. Messenger offers rich text to add pizzazz to your e-mail messages.

Rich text is text that contains fancy formatting, such as bold, underline, italics, varying fonts and font sizes, colors, paragraph formatting, and HTML codes in the body of your message. Rich text lets you embed images and animation within the body of the text.

You can use rich text to enhance both the appearance and functionality of your message. For example, if you received a URL in a rich-text message, you would just click on the URL to bring up the Web page it was linked to. However, if your e-mail software was incapable of handling rich-text messages, you wouldn't be able to launch the URL from within the mail message. Instead, you'd have to type that URL within your browser to get to its Web page.

Before you consider using rich text to compose a message to send to someone, you need to make sure that the recipient's e-mail software can display rich text messages. If your recipient doesn't have rich text capability, then your fancy rich text messages won't be displayed the way you create them, in all their colorful glory and artistic fonts. Instead they appear as if they had been created using simple ASCII text. They may even show up at the other end with a bunch of garbage within them, especially if you insert images into your message. You should always check with your recipient before sending a message laden down with rich text.

Just to show you the power of rich text, the following figure shows a message that contains an image, a hyperlink, and a table.

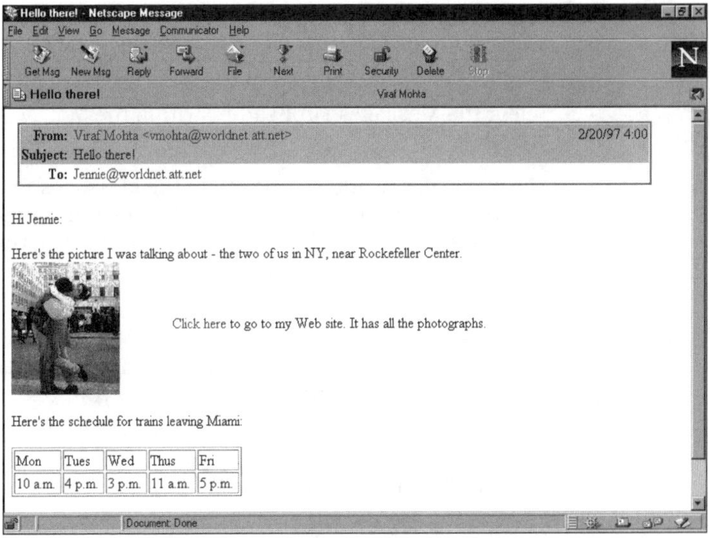

Setting Messenger up for rich text

To compose a message using rich text, you first need to make sure that Messenger has been set up properly. By default, Messenger is set up for handling rich text messages, so everything should be working fine. But just in case someone messes with your settings, here's how you set up Messenger to handle rich text messages:

1. Choose Edit⇨Preferences. The Preferences dialog box appears.

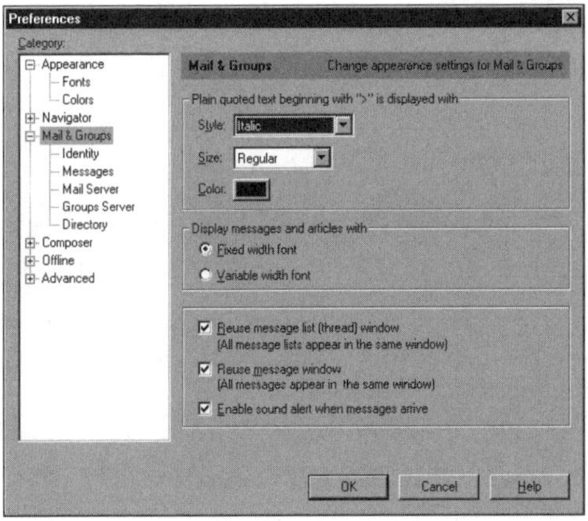

2. In the Category section, expand the Mail & Groups heading by either double-clicking on it or by clicking once on the + sign to the left of it.
3. Select the Messages subheading within the Mail & Groups heading.

   The Messages window appears. In the Messages Properties section, make sure that the option By default, send HTML messages is selected. If it is not selected, click in the check box next to the option.
4. Click on OK.

You're now set to use the rich text features in Messenger. This means you can add bold, italics, underline to your text. You can also insert pictures and URLs within your messages.

Adding bold, italics, underline, and color to your text

When plain text isn't enough to tell the full story, you can add bold, italics, underlines, and color to your text in an e-mail message:

1. Start a new message within Messenger by clicking on the New Msg button.
2. Type the text of your message.
3. Highlight the text you want to add bold, italics, underline, or color to, and then click one of the following buttons on the Rich Text toolbar:

   - To bold your text, click on the bold **A**.
   - To italicize your text, click on the italicized ***A***.
   - To underline your text, click on the underlined **A**.
   - To add color to text, click on the color selection box to the left of the bold **A**. A color palette appears. Click on a color box.

Adding a URL to your message

Adding a URL to a message gives the recipient of your message an immediate link to the Web site you discuss in your message. No more does the reader have to cut and paste the URL to the browser. Messenger acts as the browser, allowing the reader to access the Web site from within the body of the message.

You can add the URL anywhere in your message. Just follow these steps:

1. Position the cursor where you want the URL to appear.
2. Click on the Insert Object button on the Rich Text toolbar.
3. Select the Insert/Make Link from the drop-down menu that appears. The Character Properties dialog box appears displaying the Link tab, as shown in the following figure.

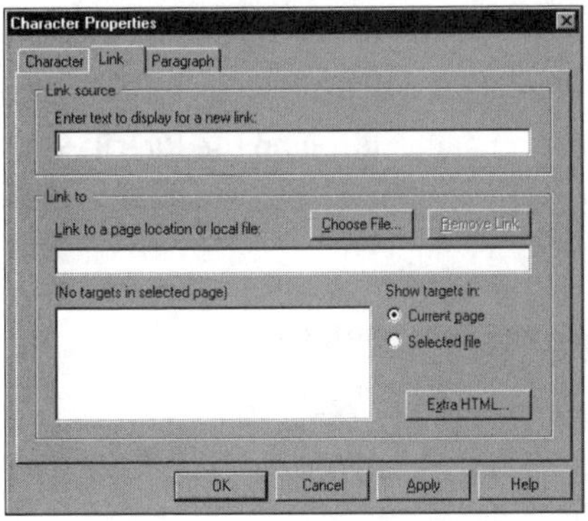

4. In the Enter text to display for a new link box, type the text which you'd like to appear as the link within the body of your message. For example, if you're adding a link to the CNN Web site, you would type something like CNN on the Web.
5. In the Link to a page location or local file box, type the URL for the Web site you want to include in your message. For example, if you want to link to the CNN Web site, you can type **http://www.cnn.com**. ***Note:*** Typing the *http://* before the URL is important.
6. Click on OK.

The URL appears in the message.

You can confirm that the URL you typed is correct by right-clicking on it and choosing Browse to from the menu that appears. Browse to in the menu should have the URL typed next to it in parentheses. If you don't connect to the URL you expect to, check the URL and make the necessary changes as follows:

1. Right-click on the URL within the Composition window.
2. Choose Link Properties from the menu.

The Character Properties window appears. Make the necessary changes.

3. Click on OK.

Adding an image to your message

Adding an image to your message adds some color to the picture. But esthetics may not be the only reason to use this feature. Don't forget that a picture is worth a thousand words. Instead of writing a paragraph describing an image, you can save space and time by adding the image to the message. You may also find that images also make the message far more effective in getting your point across to the reader.

Here's how you'd go about adding an image to your message:

1. Click on the Insert Image button on the Rich Text toolbar.
2. Choose Insert Image from the drop-down menu. The Image Properties dialog box appears.

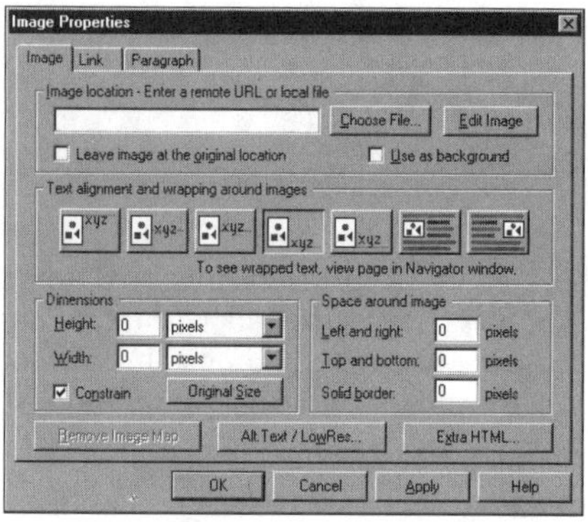

3. In the Image location box, type the location of the image file you wish to include in the message. If the image is on the Web, type its URL. If the image is on your computer, type the exact path (including the name) of the image file.

TIP

If you're not sure where your image is located, you can click on Choose File to make the Choose Image File window appear.

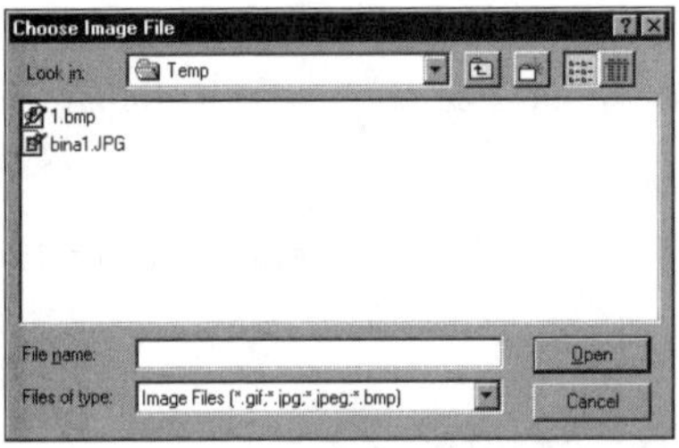

Locate the file and click on Open to transfer the filename and its path to the Image location box.

4. If you don't care about how the text of your message appears around the image, click on OK. If you do care about the way the text in the message should wrap around the image, or the size of your image as it appears in the message, then make use of some formatting options.

   Select a text alignment format by clicking on the appropriate button in the Text alignment or wrapping around images box. (The icons in the box show you what each alignment option looks like.)

   Use the Dimensions options to specify the height and width of your image. You can specify the dimensions either in pixels, or in terms of the percentage of the message screen which the image should occupy. For example, if you specify the width of the image to be 100 percent, the image will cover the entire width of the message screen.

   Use the Space around image option to leave some empty space around the image in case you have text next to the image. The space is measured in pixels. In case you're wondering how big a pixel is, here's an estimate: 100 pixels measure about an inch. You can also add a solid border around the image if necessary. To do so, specify the width of the border, also in pixels.

5. Click on OK.

Changing the font type and font size

Messenger gives you a choice of 25 fonts and more than 45 colors and shades.

To change your text to a different font:

1. Highlight the text whose font you want to change.
2. Click on the Font Selection box on the Rich Text toolbar.
3. From the drop-down menu that appears, click on the font you wish to use.

To change the size of the font in your text:

1. Highlight the text whose size you want to change.
2. Click on the Font Size Selection box on the Rich Text toolbar.
3. From the drop-down menu that appears, click on the size you wish to use.

Locating Text within Messages

Have you ever misfiled an important e-mail message? You can use the Messenger Search function to sift through all the messages in all your folders to find the message.

Here's how you can locate your lost messages:

1. Choose Edit⇨Search Messages. The Search Messages dialog box appears where you can specify what it is that you're searching for. For example, if you're looking for a message that contains a reference to Miami, the dialog box would look like this:

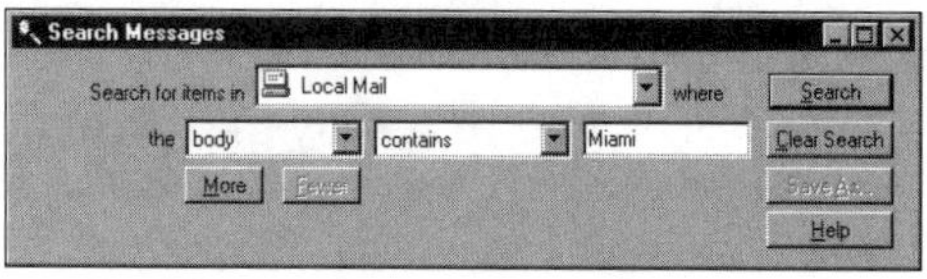

2. Specify what you want Messenger to find for you. Use the arrows next to the first three boxes to tell Messenger where to search, and then type in an appropriate keyword in the fourth box.
3. Click on Search. Messenger begins a search through the specified folders and displays the search results.

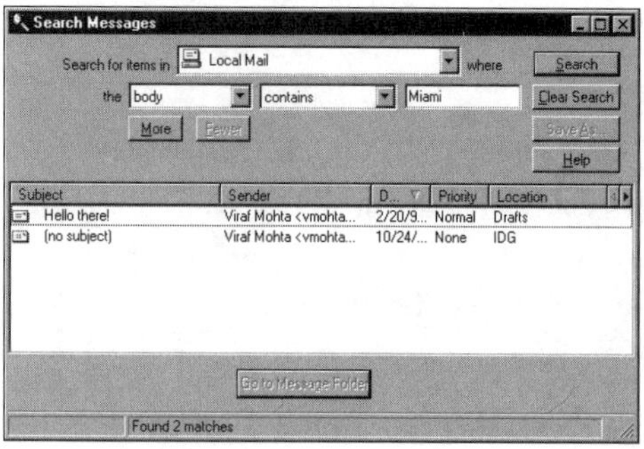

To view a message, double-click on it. To begin a new search, click on Clear Search.

Looking Up a Friend's E-Mail Address

Here's how you use directory information from within Messenger to look up a long lost pal's e-mail address:

1. Choose Edit⇨Search Directory. The Search window appears.
2. Using the drop-down menus in the various boxes, provide the necessary information for the search. Experiment with the different options to find the best set of criteria for your search.

   The following figure is an example of searching for a friend named Jennifer Bhathena in the Four11 Directory.

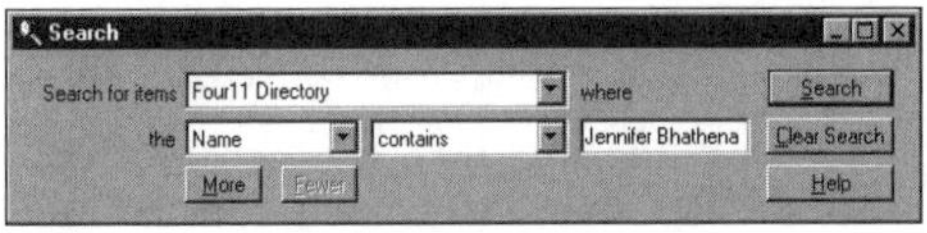

3. Click on More to provide additional boxes in which you can add more options from the preceding table to narrow the search results.

   The following figure shows an example of using the More option to provide additional information to narrow your search.

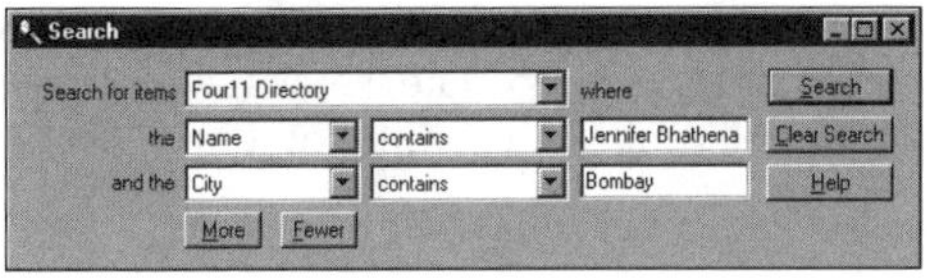

4. Click on Search. If the search directory locates individuals who meet your search criteria, Messenger displays their e-mail addresses. Double-click on any of the names listed for detailed information on that individual.

   Click on Add to Address Book if you choose to add the individual to your Personal Address Book within Messenger.

   If your search fails in finding anybody meeting your specified criteria, click on Clear Search in the Search window to begin a new search.

TIP

Search results vary between the various directories you can search, with some providing more in-depth information than others. The number of results vary, too. So if you're not successful in finding what you're looking for with one directory, try another.

Organizing Your Messages with Folders

A folder within Messenger is much like a regular folder in your file cabinet, in which you store bills, recipes, documents, and so on. Except, in Messenger, you store e-mail messages within folders. You can have a folder in which you store only messages related to your job and another for storing only messages from friends. You can have as many folders as you like.

Creating a new folder

To create a new folder:

1. Choose File⇨New Folder to open the New Folder dialog box.
2. Type the name of the folder you're creating in the Name box.
3. In the Create as subfolder of box, choose an existing folder to which you would like to add the newly created folder. If you don't want to create this new folder as a subfolder, just choose Local Mail.
4. Click on OK.

Deleting a folder

Deleting a folder is very easy:

1. Click on the Message Center icon under the Netscape 'N' logo to the far right of the screen. The Netscape Message Center window appears listing the existing folders.
2. Right-click on the folder you want to delete.
3. Choose Delete Folder from the menu that appears.

Note: You can't delete the Inbox, Drafts, and Trash folders.

Renaming a folder

Renaming a folder takes all of 30 seconds:

1. Click on the Message Center icon under the Netscape 'N' logo to the far right of the screen. The Netscape Message Center window appears listing the existing folders.
2. Right-click on the folder you want to rename.
3. Choose Rename Folder from the menu that appears. The Rename Folder window appears.
4. Type the new name for the folder in the box provided and click on OK.

Your folder appears in the folder list with its new name.

Printing a Message

To print a message:

1. Double-click the message to open it.
2. Choose File⇨Print. The Print dialog box appears.

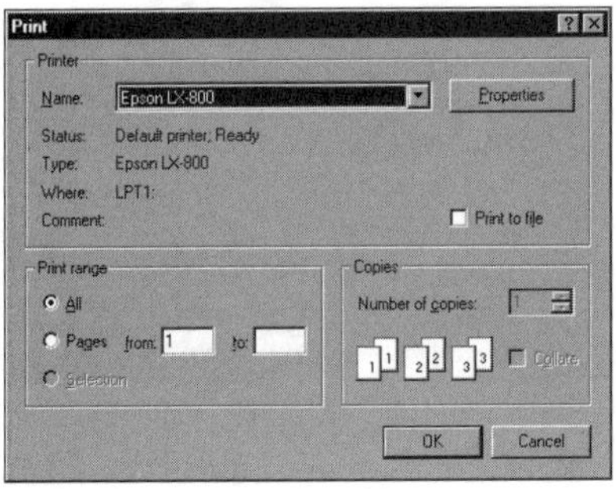

3. Specify any preferences you have about your printing job, such as specific pages you wish to print or the number of copies you want.
4. Click on OK.

Reading E-Mail

To read your e-mail, just follow these steps:

1. Launch Messenger by clicking the Mailbox icon on the Component bar, or choose Communicator⇨Messenger Mailbox. The Messenger window appears:

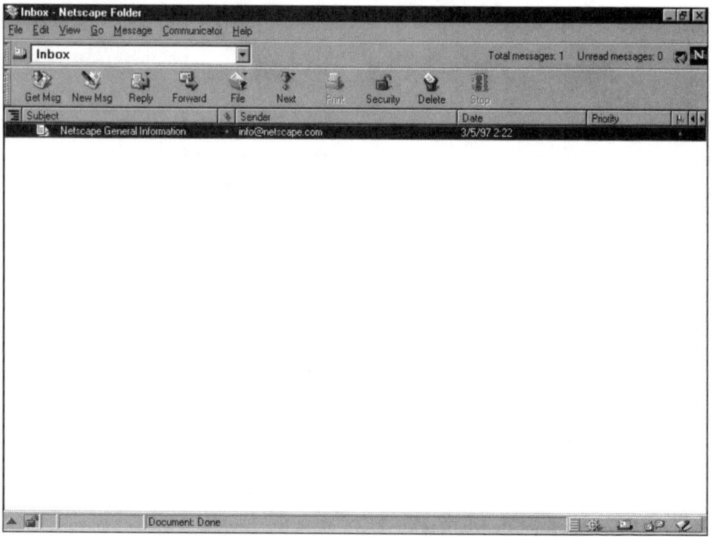

2. Clicking on Get Msg in the toolbar begins downloading your new mail from the mail server to your Inbox. A status window shows the progress of the download and tells you when the download has been completed.

3. Make the Inbox folder the active folder by clicking on the Message Center icon and then double-clicking on Inbox in the folder list.

   You see all the messages within the Inbox folder. New messages appear in bold type, with the New Message icon in the left margin.

4. Select the message you want to read by double-clicking on it. The message opens, begging you to read its text.

   To read the next message in the Inbox, click on Next on the Messenger toolbar. After reading the next message, you can return to the previous message by choosing Go⇨Back.

5. To close a message after reading it, click on the Close icon (which has an X on it) on the title bar of the message.

Replying to a Message

Follow these steps to reply to an e-mail message:

1. Highlight the message you want to reply to by clicking on it once.

2. Click on Reply on the Messenger toolbar.

3. Select one of the following two options that appear on the drop-down menu:

   - **Reply to Sender:** Your reply will be sent only to the sender of the message you're replying to.
   - **Reply to Sender and All Recipients:** Your reply will be sent to everybody who received the message you're replying to. In other words, everybody who was on the To and Cc lines of the original message will get copies of your reply.

   The Composition window appears, with the text of the message you're replying to automatically inserted in the text area of the window so that the reader of your message can refer to the text of the original message while reading your reply.

4. Type the text of your message in the text area of the Composition window.

5. Click on Send.

Saving a Message to Your Hard Disk

At times, you may receive a message that you you'll want to file away for future reference. To prevent accidentally deleting this message from your Messenger folder, you should consider making a copy of it on your hard disk.

To save messages to your hard disk:

1. Select the message from the message list by clicking on it once.

2. Choose File⇨Save As. The Save Messages As window appears.

   You can save the message in HTML format or in plain text format. If the page has any HTML formatted material in it, such as URLs, images, bulleted lists, or tables, I recommend that you save it in HTML format. If it doesn't have any of this HTML formatted material in it, you can save it in plain text format.

   To save it in HTML format, select HTML Files in the Save as type box. To save it in plain text format, select Plain text (*.txt) in the Save as type box.

3. Give the file a name which is a little more descriptive than the default name *untitled.html,* which appears in the File name box. You'll thank me for this. Specify the folder you want to save the message to in the Save in box.

4. Click on Save. Your message is now saved on your computer.

Part IV

Netscape Collabra

About 16,000 newsgroups, focusing on topics as diverse as acting and Zoroastrianism, exist. These newsgroups collectively form a portion of the Internet called *Usenet*. Some newsgroups are monitored for language and content, while others allow a virtual free-for-all mentality.

Regardless of the approach they follow, newsgroups can provide a wealth of information. Netscape Collabra, the Communicator newsgroup reader, allows you to tap into this rich source of information.

You can also host discussion groups similar to Usenet newsgroups on your company intranet, allowing employees to air their views, discuss projects, and contribrute to policy making. Participating in these discussion groups is similar to participating in Usenet newsgroups on the Internet, the only difference being that the intranet discussion groups are available to company employees only.

In this part . . .

- **Discovering newsgroups and news servers**
- **Subscribing and unsubscribing to newsgroups**
- **Composing newsgroup posts**
- **Following message threads and replying to posts**
- **Filing, copying, and saving posts**
- **Printing posts**

Choosing News Servers

A *news server* is a computer tucked away in a little room somewhere in your company, or at your Internet Service Provider's offices — if you use an ISP to connect to the Internet — through which you, a user, access newsgroups. If you're connected to the Internet via your employer's Internet connection, you're connected to your employer's news server. The ISP (your employer) stores the contents of newsgroups on news servers.

An ISP may choose to carry only a selected number of newgroups. As a user, you're limited to only those newsgroups which are available on the news server you have connected to. Disk space availability on a news server and the nature of a particular newsgroup usually determine whether or not an ISP will carry a newsgroup. For example, many employers feel it is unprofessional to carry newsgroups on which adult or pornographic material is discussed.

Checking your news server connection

Collabra may not be set up for receiving news from a news server. To ensure that it is, do the following:

1. Choose Edit⇨Preferences. The Preferences window appears.
2. Double-click on the Mail & Groups category to expand it, if it isn't already expanded. You see components listed within the Mail & Groups category.
3. Click on the Groups Server component in the Mail & Groups category. The Groups Server dialog box appears.

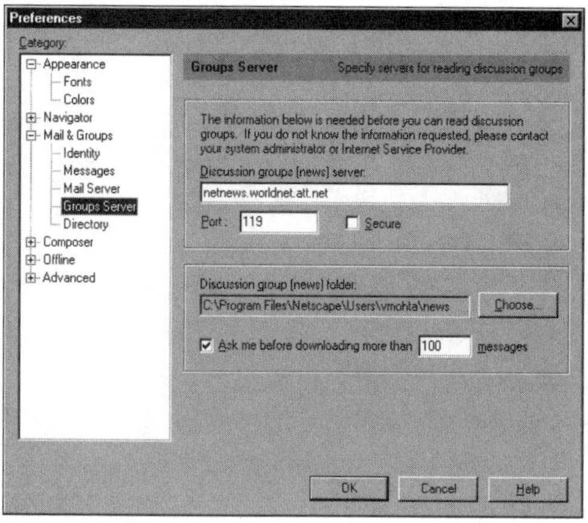

4. If the Discussion groups (news) server box is empty, you're not connected to a news server. In that case, you need to contact the local computer guru in your office or the Systems Administrator to get the name of the news server that you should type in that box. If your Internet connection is through an ISP, contact the ISP and get the name of the news server from them.

Adding a news server

Numerous news servers exist on the Internet, many of which cater to very specific discussions or topics. You have the liberty to connect to a whole bunch of them, giving you a wide selection of discussions and topics to choose from and participate in.

To add a news server, you must first know the exact name of the server and the port to which it is connected. You can get this information from your ISP. After you have this information:

1. Choose File⇨New Discussion Groups Server. The New Discussions Groups Server window appears.
2. Type the name of the news server in the Server box.
3. Click on the Secure check box if the server is secure. A *secure server* is one which limits access to certain individuals only, via a name and password check. Most servers are not secure. If this news server that you're adding is a secure server, your Systems Administrator or ISP will let you know that it is.
4. Click on OK.

Collabra now adds the news server to your list of news servers. You should see it listed in the Netscape Message Center window, at the bottom of the folder list. You can now start adding newsgroups to your list of things to read.

Deleting a news server

Have you ever subscribed to a magazine, only to find that you never get time to read it? Don't be surprised if you never get the time to read what's on the news servers you subscribed to, either.

Just like cancelling a magazine subscription, you may at some point want to delete a news server from your list of subscribed servers. This is how you do it:

1. In the Message Center window, right-click on the news server you want to delete.
2. From the menu that appears, choose Remove Discussion Group Server. You see a message asking if you really, really want to remove that news server from your list.

3. Click on Yes. That news server will never bother you again (unless you reconnect to it).

Switching to newsgroups on other news servers

Because some news servers don't carry all possible newsgroups, you may need to switch news servers during your Collabra sessions in order to participate in discussions carried on other news servers. You can jump from one news server to another by following these steps:

1. Double-click on the news server you want to switch. All the discussion groups subscribed to on that news server appear.
2. Double-click on the group you wish to go to. The message headers from that group appear.
3. Click on a message header to read the contents of that message. The contents of the message appear in the lower half of the discussion window.
4. To exit from that discussion group, choose File⇨Close.

If a group you wish to go to isn't listed within the news server, you can subscribe to the newsgroup and thereby permanently add it to the news server. To do so:

1. Right-click on the subscribed news server you want to switch to.
2. From the menu that appears, choose Subscribe to Discussion Groups. The Communicator: Subscribe to Discussion Groups dialog box appears.

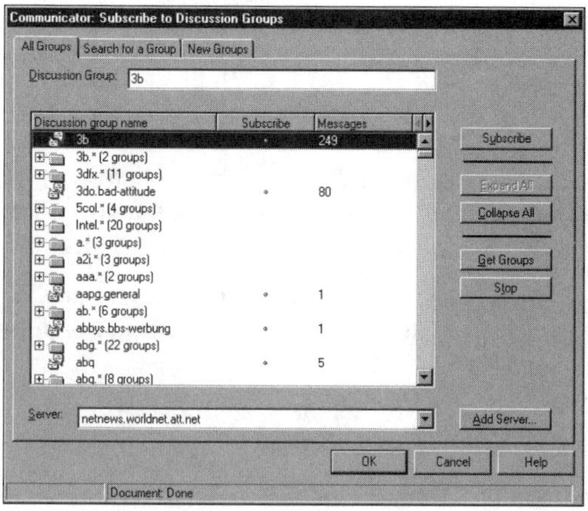

A few seconds later, or longer, depending on your Internet connection, you see a list of all the newsgroups available on that news server.

3. Click on the group you wish to subscribe to.
4. Click on the group you wish to subscribe to, but this time on the little dot that you see to the right of the group name, in the Subscribe column.
5. Click on OK. This returns you to the Netscape Message Center window. The newsgroup you subscribed to should now be available as an option within the news server heading you had selected. If it's not visible, it's because the news server heading is not expanded. Double-click on the news server to display all subscribed discussion groups within it.
6. Double-click on the group you wish to go to.
7. Click on a message header to read the contents of that message. The contents appear in the lower half of the discussion window.
8. To exit from that discussion group, choose File➪Close.

Marking a Post

Because a single newsgroup can contain thousands of posts, keeping track of a specific post makes it easier to come back to the post during your session. You can tag the post with a flag, making it easier to find. Think of marking posts as dropping bread crumbs as you read your way through a newsgroup. Just follow these steps to mark your posts:

1. Click on the post you want to mark or tag.
2. Choose Message➪Flag Message. You should now see a little orange flag on the message summary line, toward the right edge of the window in the column marked with a flag.

Message marked with a flag

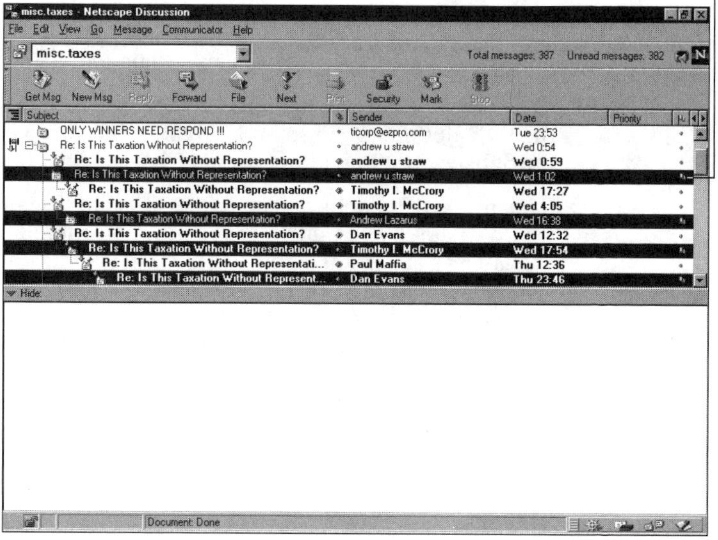

To remove the flag:

1. Click on the post you want to "unmark" or "untag."
2. Choose Message⇨Unflag Message.

Posting Messages to a Newsgroup

Online and offline discussions are similiar in one important respect: You need to listen to the coversation before you jump in and start talking yourself.

After you read a newsgroup for a while and get a feel for the type of coversation that takes place there, you may want to post a message or two to the newsgroup. Collabra takes the bite out of participating in online discussions by making posting a message as easy as watching ice melt.

You can either create a new post of your own to post on a newsgroup, or you can reply to a someone else's post on the newsgroup.

Creating a new message to post on a newsgroup

Repeat after me: "I will post a message to a newsgroup only if I have something worthwhile to say." Way too many people clutter up newsgroups with messages which have little meaning. With that out of the way, you can get on with the show.

While you are reading a newsgroup, you can create a new message to post by following these steps:

1. Click on New Msg on the toolbar. The Message Composition window appears.

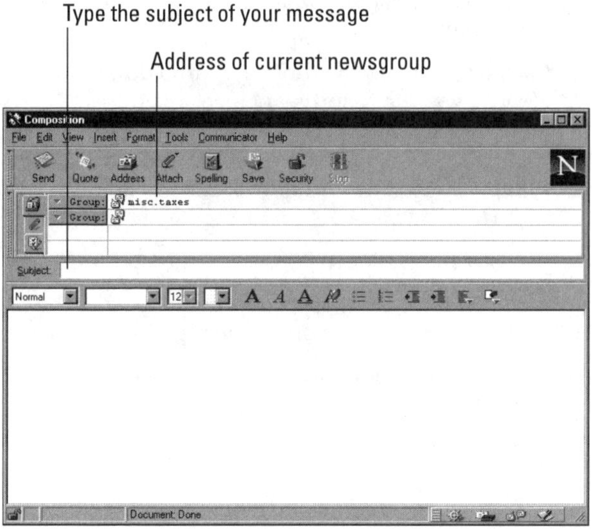

Notice that the name of the current newsgroup automatically appears in the Group box.

2. Type a Subject for your post so readers can tell what your post is about.

3. Type your post.

4. Click on Send.

TIP

If you really want to get fancy with your posts, you can use *rich text* to liven things up. Rich text lets you add all kinds of fancy-shmancy things to your posts, including colorful images, blinking and dancing animations, and HTML links. In plain text, your text is plain vanilla. ***See also*** "Spicing Up Your Posts with Rich Text" in this part.

However, rich text posts can be read only by those who have the ability to do so via a news reader such as Collabra. The majority of users on the Internet still lack this capability, so it's best to stick to plain text posts unless you're posting on an Intranet discussion group on which a majority of users may use a rich text news reader like Collabra.

Responding to a newsgroup post

Sometimes you may want to contribute your two cents to an existing post on a newsgroup. When you feel the time is right, just follow these steps to make your voice heard:

1. Click on the post you want to reply to. The contents of the post appear.
2. Click on Reply on the toolbar. A drop-down menu appears offering you the following choices to address your reply:
   - Reply to the Sender of the message only.
   - Reply to the Sender of the message and to all recepients of the message.
   - Post your response on the newsgroup only.
   - Send a reply to the person who the posted the message *and* post your response on the newsgroup too.
3. Choose who you want to send your reply to. The Message Composition window appears.
4. Type your post.
5. Click on Send.

Your post is on its way.

TIP: Don't be surprised if the post you send to a newsgroup doesn't show up immediately. It usually takes a couple of hours, sometimes longer, for your message to be posted.

Printing a Post

Sometime you want to take a post with you to a meeting, or maybe even hang it up on your refrigerator door. You can print out a post by following these steps:

1. In the Message List, click on the post you want to print.
2. Choose File⇨Print. The Print dialog box appears.

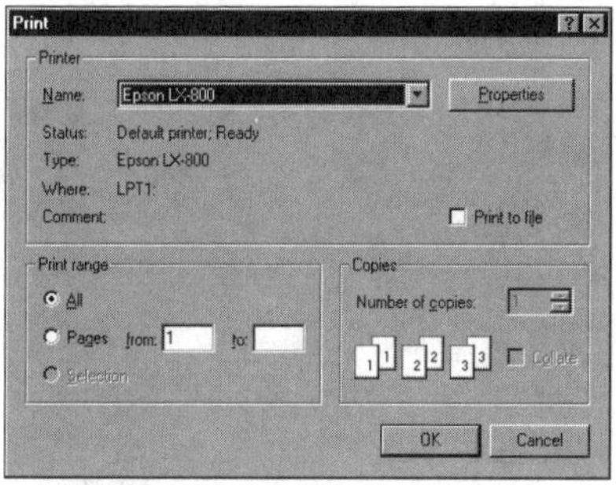

3. Specify any appropriate printing options, such as the number of copies you want.
4. Click on OK.

Reading a Newsgroup

Newsgroups often contain thousands of posts. Can you imagine yourself scrolling up and down the message list trying to link a post you just read with replies to it, *if* there are any? I don't know about you, but I've better things to do.

It's a lot easier to follow a discussion if all related posts are grouped together. In other words, if all the posts pertaining to a particular topic are *threaded,* or linked, together. A *thread* is a group of posts that discuss the same topic. Collabra arranges posts in a thread hierarchically in the Netscape Discussion window.

For example, if I post a message on a newsgroup asking for opinions about taxation, all suggestions posted in response to my query form a message thread. You could then follow this thread to see what people have suggested, thereby keeping this discussion separate from all others going on on the newsgroup at the same time.

Click on a message to read it

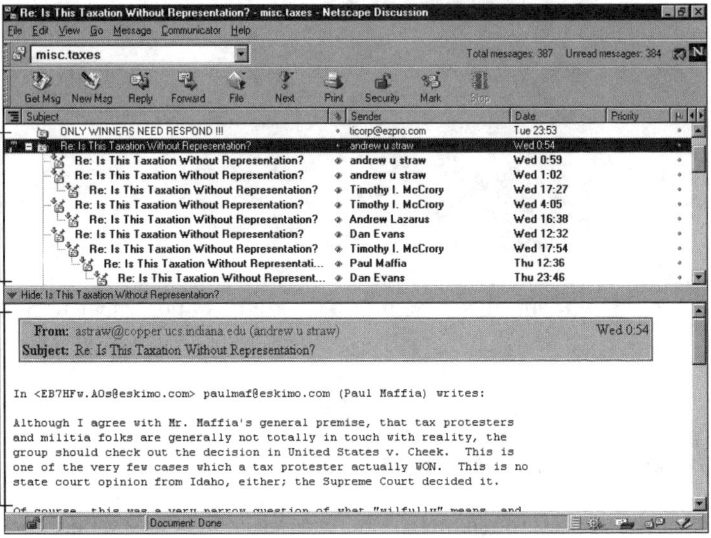

Read the message

To get in on the action of reading threaded message newsgroups, follow these steps:

1. In the Message Center, list the newsgroups within a news server by clicking on the + sign next to the news server name. A list of all the newsgroups you subscribe to appears.

2. Double-click on a newsgroup you want to read.

   If the number of messages within a newsgroup is greater than the download limit set in the Collabra Preferences settings (***see also*** "Setting a Limit for the Number of Messages Being Downloaded"), Collabra displays a dialog box titled Download Headers, offering you the option of downloading only a specific number of messages, thereby saving you time on a slow modem connection. On a 28.8 modem connection, you should download about 100 messages at a time. If the Download Headers dialog box appears when you download messages, select the number of headers (messages) you wish to download and then click on Download.

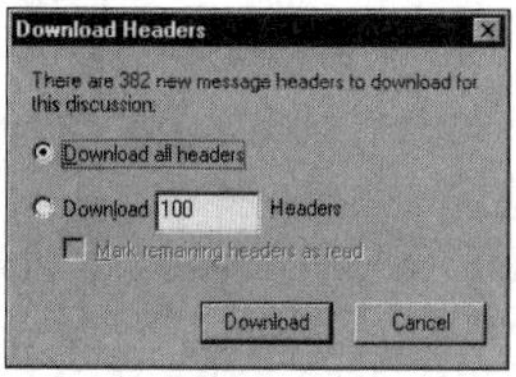

If the number of messages within the newsgroup is less than the limit specified in the Collabra Preferences settings, Collabra downloads all the messages within the newsgroup.

The Netscape Discussion window for the newsgroup appears, with the message headers listed within it.

The top part of the window lists the messages in the newsgroup; the bottom part lists the contents of the message selected in the top window. Each time you select a new message in the Netscape Discussion window, the contents of the bottom window change accordingly.

3. To read a post, click on the post. The post's contents appear in the lower half of the screen.

To display only new posts within threads or new posts posted to the newsgroup, choose View⇨Messages⇨New.

To download another batch of messages from the newsgroup, choose File⇨Get Messages⇨Next 100. The number next to Next is the maximum number of messages set by you within the Collabra Preferences options.

Saving a Post to Your Disk

When you come across (or write) a post that you want to save for posterity, you can save a post either into a personal folder (***see also*** "Saving Newsgroup Posts into Folders"), or you can or save it on a hard disk or floppy disk.

Saving a post to your hard disk or floppy disk differs from filing the post within a folder in a Message Center folder. When you save a post to your hard disk or floppy disk, the post can be later viewed and edited using your favorite word-processor just like you would any other file. Filing a post within a folder, on the other hand, saves it using a different format. The format resembles a database in which several items are stored, the items being the posts. Collabra stores the posts in a single file, but the posts can be viewed as individual items.

To save a post to your hard disk:

1. In the Netscape Discussion window, right-click on the post that you want to save.
2. In the menu that appears, choose Save Message. The Save Messages As dialog box appears.

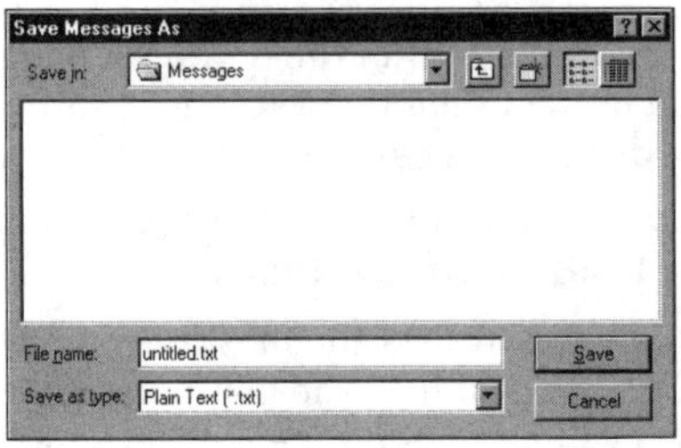

You can save the post in HTML format or in Plain Text format. If the page has any HTML formatted material in it, such as URLs, images, bulleted lists, or tables, you may wish to retain those features by saving the post in HTML format. If it doesn't have any of this HTML formatted material in it, you can save it in Plain Text format.

3. To save a post in HTML format, select HTML Files in the Save as type box. To save it in Plain Text format, select Plain Text (*.txt) in the Save as type box.
4. Give the file a name which is a little more descriptive than untitled.html. You'll thank me for this later after you have saved tons of posts.
5. Click on Save.

Saving Newsgroup Posts into Folders

You can file a post from a newsgroup for future reference. Due to the sheer number of posts you can read in a newsgroup, you may soon appreciate being able to file just the ones you want to keep into a folder.

If you don't yet have a folder set aside to hold your newsgroup posts, you can create one by following these steps:

1. Right-click on the Local Mail button within the Message Center.
2. From the menu that appears, choose New Folder. You see the New Folder dialog box.

3. Type a name for the new folder in the Name box.
4. Click on OK.

To file a post from a newsgroup to a folder, just breeze right through these steps:

1. Right-click on the post header within the newsgroup.
2. From the menu that appears, choose File Message. Yet another menu listing the folders on your machine appears.
3. Choose a folder to file the post in. Collabra files your post into the folder you choose.

Searching for a Post within a Newsgroup

Sometimes you want to look up some information that you may have read in a post, but you just don't remember which of the gazillion (how many millions in a gazillion?) posts within the newsgroup you had seen that information in.

Of course, the easiest way to remember a particular post is to mark the post. ***See also*** "Marking a Post" in this part.

But if you forget to mark that all-important post, you can still pull it up, as long as you remember something specific about the post, such as the date, subject, name of sender, or even a word or phrase in the text of the post.

Here's how you find the post you've been looking for:

1. Choose Edit⇨Search Messages. A search window pops up on your screen. This is where you specify what you're looking for.

   For example, if you're looking for a post in the `misc.taxes` newgroup from a particular sender, your search form would look something like this:

2. Click on Search. Collabra begins a search through the current newsgroup and displays the search results.

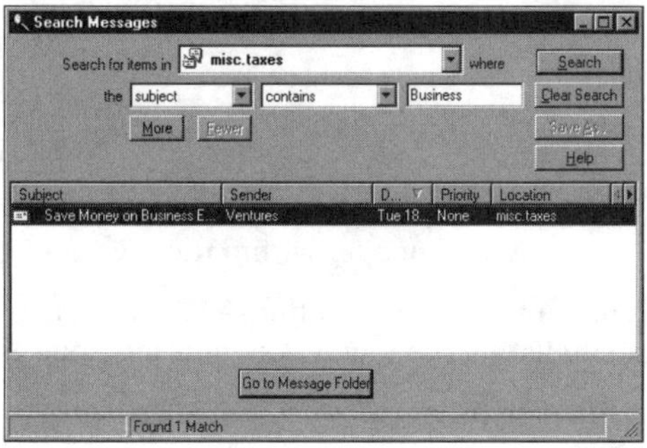

Collabra searches are *case-sensitive*, meaning that a search on *Business* may not produce the same results as a search on *business*.

To view a post that Collabra pulls up as a result of your search, just double-click on the post. To begin a new search, click on Clear Search.

Setting a Limit for Downloaded Messages

Some newsgroups have thousands of messages within them. Downloading all these messages can easily take a few hours on a modem connection.

Collabra allows you to specify the maximum number of messages to be downloaded from a newsgroup. If the number of messages on the newsgroup you've selected is greater than the maximum number you specify, Collabra alerts you of this and lets you specify the number of messages you want to download at that time.

Follow these steps if you want Collabra to tell you if the number of posts you want to download from a newsgroup exceeds a certain number:

1. Choose Edit⇨Preferences. The Preferences window appears.
2. Double-click on the Mail & Groups category to expand it, if the category isn't already expanded. You see the components listed within the Mail & Groups category.
3. Click on the Groups Server component in the Mail & Groups category. The window now displays the current settings for the Groups Server.

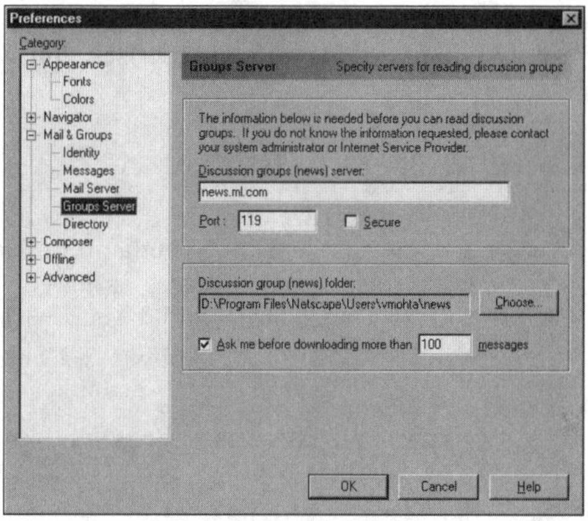

4. If there is no check mark in the box next to Ask me before downloading, click on it.

5. In the box next to messages, type the maximum number of messages you want Collabra to download without having to alert you.

6. Click on OK.

Now Collabra will alert you any time you connect to a newsgroup in which there are more messages than the maximum limit you've specified.

In the preceding figure, the contents of the Discussion Groups (news) server and the Discussion groups (news) folder will be different from that which appears on your screen. That's only because you and I use different news servers and news folders.

Spicing Up Your Posts with Rich Text

Using rich text in your posts lets you add cool stuff, like formatting, Web site addresses, and animation to your newgroup posts.

Although your posts look way cool compared to those created using just plain text, you should know that the majortiy of Internet users don't have the ability to view rich text posts yet. Those users see just plain text in black instead of the fancy fonts and bright colors you may have used. Additionally, the images you may have added to your post show up as nothing more than garbled text.

Unless you're sure that the readers of the newsgroup you're posting to have the ability to view rich text posts, you should post using plain text.

Setting Collabra up to use rich text

To compose a post using rich text, you first need to make sure that Collabra has been set up properly. By default, Collabra is set up for handling rich text posts, so everything should be working fine. But if some buttinsky comes along and messes with your settings, you need to know how to get them into working order again:

1. Choose Edit⇨Preferences. The Preferences window appears.

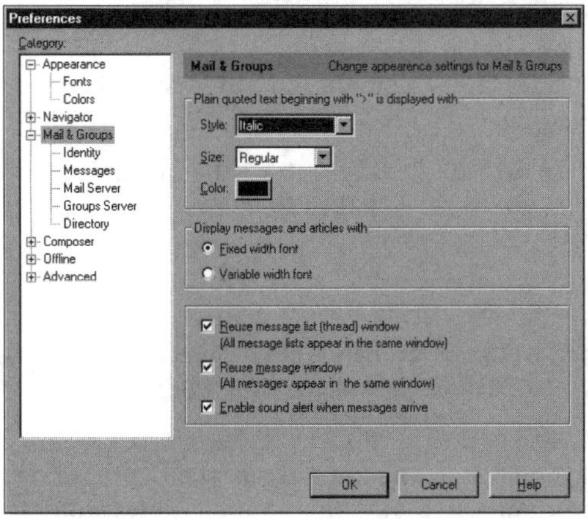

2. Expand the Mail & Groups heading by either double-clicking on it or by clicking on the + sign to the left of it.
3. Select the Messages subheading within the Mail & Groups heading. The Messages dialog box appears.
4. In the Messages Properties section, make sure that there is a checkmark for the option By default, send HTML messages. If there isn't one, click on the box next to the option.
5. Click on OK.

You're now set to use the rich text features in Collabra.

Formatting your posts

Nothing adds emphasis to your words more effectively than formatting. Adding bold, italics, underlines, and color to your posts is very easy. Here's how you do it:

1. Create the post you want to format. ***See also*** "Posting Messages to a Newsgroup" in this part.

2. Use the Formatting toolbar to format the text in your post that you want to emphasize.

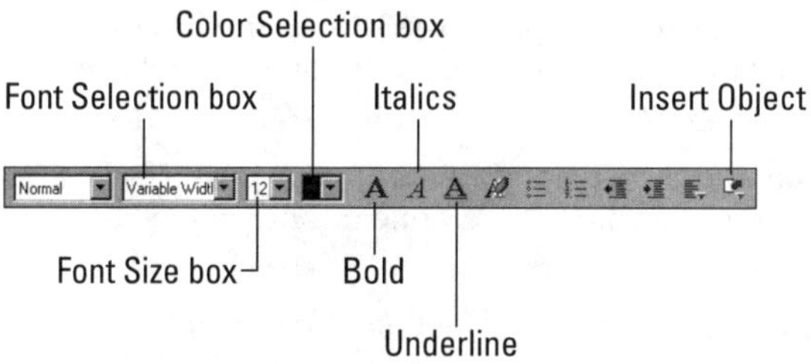

To bold the text, highlight the text and then click on the bold **A** on the Formatting toolbar.

To italicize the text, highlight the text and then click on the italicized ***A*** on the Formatting toolbar.

To underline the text, highlight the text and then click on the underlined **A** on the Formatting toolbar.

To add color to text, highlight the text and then click on the Color Selection box on the Formatting toolbar. A color palette appears. Click on a color box. The highlighted text should now sport the new color.

You can also completely change the font of your text. Collabra gives you a choice of 25 fonts.

To change your text to a different font:

1. Highlight the text whose font you want to change.

2. Click on the Font Selection box on the Formatting toolbar.

3. From the drop-down menu which appears, click on the font you wish to use.

The highlighted text should now have the new font.

To change the size of the font in your text:

1. Highlight the text whose size you want to change.

2. Click on the Font Size selection box on the Formatting toolbar.

3. From the drop-down menu that appears, click on the size you wish to use.

The highlighted text should now be the revised size.

Adding a Web address to your post

Adding a URL to a post gives the recipient of your post an immediate link to the Web site you discuss in your post. The reader no longer needs to cut-n-paste the URL to the browser. Collabra acts as the browser, allowing the reader access to the Web site from within the body of the post.

You can add the URL anywhere in your post. Just place the cursor where you want the URL to appear. Then follow these steps to add a URL:

1. Click on the Insert Object icon on the Formatting toolbar.
2. Select the Insert/Make Link from the drop-down menu that appears. You see the Character Properties dialog box.

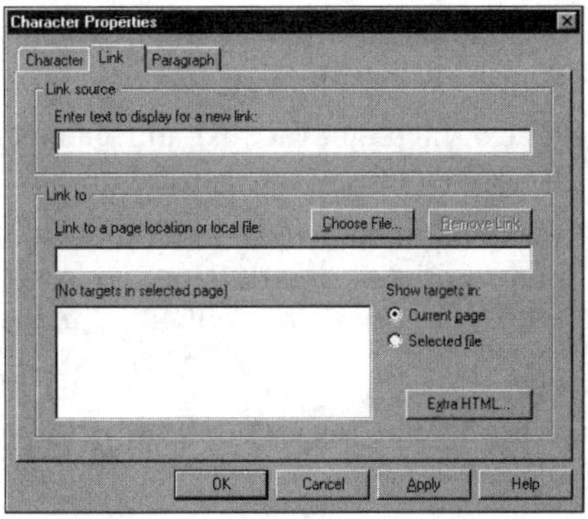

3. In the Enter text to display for a new link box, type the text which you'd like to appear as the link within the body of your post. For example, if you're adding a link to the CNN Web site, you would type something like **CNN on the Web**.
4. In the Link to a page location or local file box, type the URL for the Web site you want to include in your post. For example, if you want to link to the CNN Web site, you would type **http://www.cnn.com**. It's important to type the *http://* before the URL.
5. Click on OK.

The URL should now appear in the post.

You can confirm that the URL you typed is correct by right-clicking on it and choosing Browse to: from the menu that appears. Browse to: should have the URL typed next to it in parentheses. By choosing Browse to you should connect to the URL you typed. If you don't connect to the URL you expect to, check the URL and follow these steps to make the necessary changes:

1. Right-click on the URL within the Composition window.
2. Choose Link Properties from the menu. The Charcater Properties dialog box appears.
3. Make the necessary changes.
4. Click on OK.

Adding an image to your post

Adding an image to your post adds some color to the picture. But esthetics may not be the only reason to use this feature. Don't forget that a picture is worth a thousand words. Instead of writing a paragraph describing an image, you can save space and time by adding the image to the post. You may also find that images also make the post far more effective in getting your point across to the reader.

Here's how you'd go about adding an image to your post:

1. Click on the Insert Object button on the Formatting toolbar.
2. Choose Insert Image from the drop-down menu that appears. The Image Properties dialog box appears.

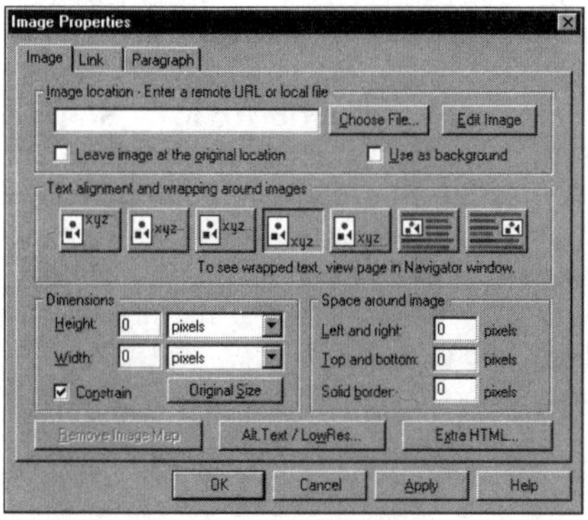

3. In the Image location box, enter the location of the image file you wish to include in the post. If the image is on the Web, type the image's URL. If the image is on your computer, type the exact path (including the name) of the image file.

   If you're not sure where your image is located, you can click on Choose File to make the Choose Image File dialog box appear.

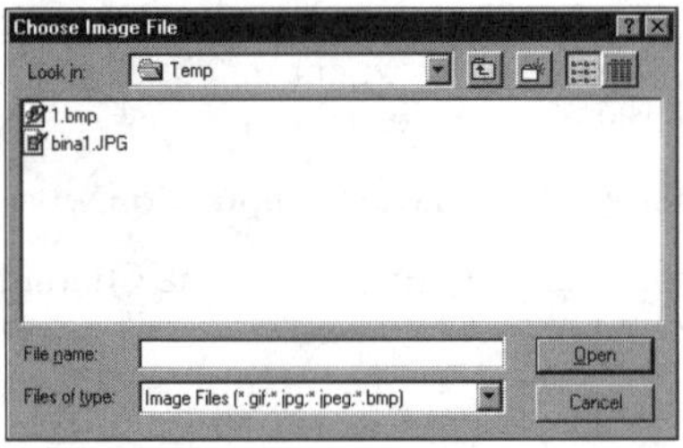

Locate the file and click on Open to transfer the filename and its path to the Image Location box.

4. If you don't care about how the text of your post appears around the image, click on OK. If you do care about the way the text in the post should wrap around the image, or the size of your image as it appears in the post, then make use of some formatting options.

   Select a text alignment format by clicking on the appropriate button in the Text alignment or wrapping around images box. (The icons in the box show you what each alignment option looks like.)

   Use the Dimensions options to specify the height and width of your image. You can specify the dimensions either in pixels, or in terms of the percentage of the post screen which the image should occupy. For example, if you specify the width of the image to be 100%, the image covers the entire width of the post screen.

   Use the Space around image option to leave some empty space around the image in case you have text next to the image. The space is measured in pixels. In case you're wondering how big a pixel is, here's an estimate. One hundred pixels add up to about an inch. You can also add a solid border around the image if necessary. To do so, specify the width of the border, also in pixels.

5. Click on OK.

Subscribing to a Newsgroup

A *newsgroup* is a place on the Internet where people gather to discuss a topic of common interest. A newsgroup resembles an electronic bulletin board on which people post questions or comments, and others respond to these questions and comments. Others then respond to the responses, and so on, until a string, or *thread*, of discussion about a topic emerges. At any given time, multiple discussions can be in progress in a particular newsgroup.

When you connect to a news server, you're presented with a list of all the newsgroups available on it. In some cases, the list could contain thousands of newsgroups. Each time you connect to the news server, you may need to scroll through this long list of newsgroups to get to the newsgroup you want to read. This can get pretty annoying after a while.

Instead of rooting out your newsgroup each time you want to read it, you can permanently list your newsgroup of choice in your Message Center listing, under the news server. This is what *subscribing to a newsgroup* means. Then, each time you connect to the news server, Collabra automatically connects to all subscribed newsgroups and displays the number of messages currently posted on each newsgroup.

You can subscribe to as many newsgroups as you want. Imagine how much work Collabra saves you, if you have ten newsgroups which you read everyday. In one step, you can download posts from all ten of them.

Subscribing to a newsgroup is a one-time process. After you subscribe to a newsgroup, it stays in your Message Center until you delete it.

When you know the newsgroup's name

The Internet is swimming with thousands of newsgroups, catering to every whim, fancy, and pet peeve.

TIP

To browse through a comprehensive list of all newsgroups, go to `http://sunsite.unc.edu/usenet-i/` or to `http://www.liszt.com/news`. Both these sites maintain extensive information on Usenet groups.

If you know the exact name of the newsgroup you want to subscribe to:

1. Right-click on the news server within the Message Center window.
2. From the menu that appears, choose Subscribe to Discussion Groups. The Communicator: Subscribe to Discussion Groups window appears, displaying a list of newsgroups on the server.

   As Collabra lists the newsgroups, the status bar at the bottom of the window reads Receiving discussion groups. After Collabra lists all the newsgroups, the status bar reads Document: Done.

3. In the Discussion Group box, type the name of the newsgroup you want to subscribe to. If the newsgroup exists on the server, Collabra displays the newsgroup in the window. If the newsgroup has a + sign next to it, it contains subgroups within it. Click on the + sign to display all subgroups within the newsgroup.
4. Click on the newsgroup you wish to subscribe to.
5. Click on the group you wish to subscribe to, but this time on the little dot that you see to the right of the group name, in the Subscribe column. A checkmark should now appear in place of the dot.
6. Repeat the preceding steps for all the newsgroups you want to subscribe to.
7. Click on OK. Collabra now lists the newsgroups in the Message Center, under the news server.

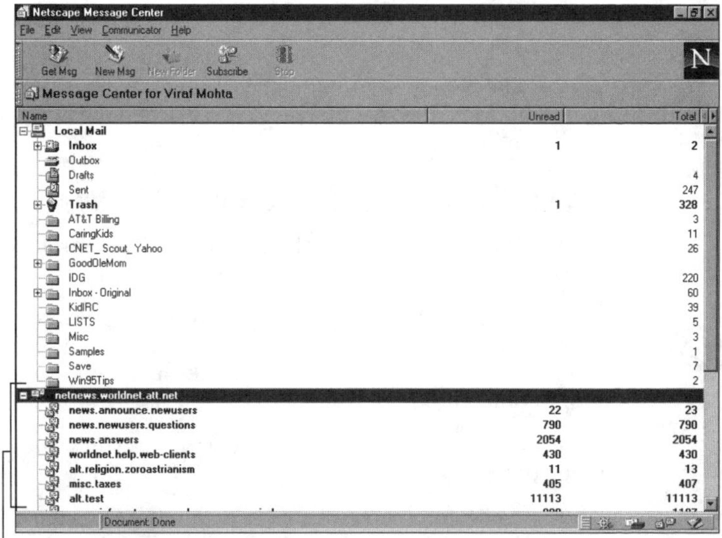

Collabra lists your newsgroups

When you don't know the name of the newsgroup

You can subscribe to a newsgroup even if you don't know what the group is called. You have to do a little hunting, but it can be done by following these steps:

1. Right-click on the news server within the Message Center window.

2. From the menu that appears, choose Subscribe to Discussion Groups. The Communicator: Subscribe to Discussion Groups window appears, showing a list of newsgroups on the server. The status bar at the bottom of the window reads Receiving discussion groups as Collabra lists the newsgroups. After Collabra finishes listing all newsgroups, the status bar reads Document: Done.

3. After all the newsgroups appear, scroll down the list until you find the newsgroup you want to subscribe to, highlight it, and click on Subscribe. The newsgroup should now appear on the folder list within the Message Center.

WARNING! Although Usenet offers 16,000 newsgroups, not all of them may be available to you. Newsgroups and the posts within them take up a lot of disk space. Hence your Internet Service Provider (ISP), or your employer, may maintain only a partial list of newsgroups on its news server. Your choice of newsgroups is limited to the newsgroups within that list. If a newsgroup you wish to subscribe to is not on that list, you may request that the Internet Administrator to add it to the list. Don't count on immediate cooperation, though.

TIP To view all the newsgroups you have subscribed to on a particular news server, double-click on the news server's name or click on the + sign to the left of the news server's name. All the newsgroups listed within the news server should appear. To hide the newsgroup list again, double-click on the news server name or click on the – sign to the left of the news server's name.

Unsubscribing a newsgroup

Even though you may have subscribed to a newsgroup, you may rarely read what's in it. So if you feel you want to unsubscribe to a newsgroup, here's what you do:

1. Right-click on the newsgroup within the Message Center window.

2. From the menu that appears, choose Remove Discussion Group. A dialog box appears asking you whether you're sure you want to unsubscribe from the newsgroup.

3. Click on Yes to zap the newsgroup.

Part V

Netscape Composer

The time may come when you tire of just cruising the Web. At some point, you may want to create a place of your very own on the Web. When that time comes, this part of the book will show you the way.

A home on the Web is called a *Web site*. And just as the house you live in may have several rooms, each Web site can have several *pages*. And just as each room within a house has to be connected to at least one other room, each page on a Web site is connected to at least one other page.

Composer has simplified creating home pages into a point-and-click routine. With the help of templates built into Composer, you can have a page ready in a matter of minutes.

In this part . . .

- **Looking at the essentials of a good page**
- **Creating a home page with the Composer toolbar**
- **Creating a home page with a template**
- **Creating a home page with the Wizard**
- **Editing a page you're viewing**
- **Previewing your home page**
- **Publishing your home page**

Acquainting Yourself with Web Page Basics

You don't need a degree in Graphic Design to come up with a well-designed page. As long as you keep the page simple and easy to read, you'll do fine. Keep the following items in mind when designing pages and your pages will turn out user-friendly every time:

✦ **Always give your page a title:** A title lets your viewers know what they're about to see. It's like the title of a chapter that gives a reader a clue about the chapter's contents.

✦ **Limit the number of graphics:** Nothing's more irritating than spending 20 minutes waiting for the graphics on a page to download. By all means, have graphics on your page — they make the page exciting and fun — but don't go overboard and crowd your page with them.

✦ **Use small pictures:** You shouldn't use big pictures. High resolution graphics may look great, but their file size is always larger than their low-resolution version. Graphics lose their appeal if they're too big and take too long to download. Not everyone on the Web has the luxury of cruising at the high speeds available at many large corporations.

A very large number of surfers use nothing more than 28.8 modems. At peak times, downloads slow down to a crawl. So make sure your graphics are small enough for fast downloads. Try to restrict their file sizes to between 30K and 40K. That way viewers will appreaciate your graphics even more.

✦ **Provide proper links:** Hitting the Back button repeatedly to return to a particular page gets tiresome quickly. Always make sure that each page you create has adequate links on it to let a user navigate to any other page. Otherwise, the visit begins to resemble a journey through a maze.

✦ **Keep the pages short:** Limit the length of your pages to three screens. The contents of each page should be displayed completely if a user presses Page Down twice. Anything more than this forces a user to constantly scroll up and down the page, and your visitors may lose interest quickly.

Creating a Page with the Composer Toolbar

Although using the Composer toolbar gives you the least amount of assistance in developing a home page (compared to creating a home page using a template or the Netscape Wizard), you can still easily use the toolbar to create your masterpiece.

To access the Composer toolbar, just launch Composer. Your blank canvas, along with the Composer toolbar, appears.

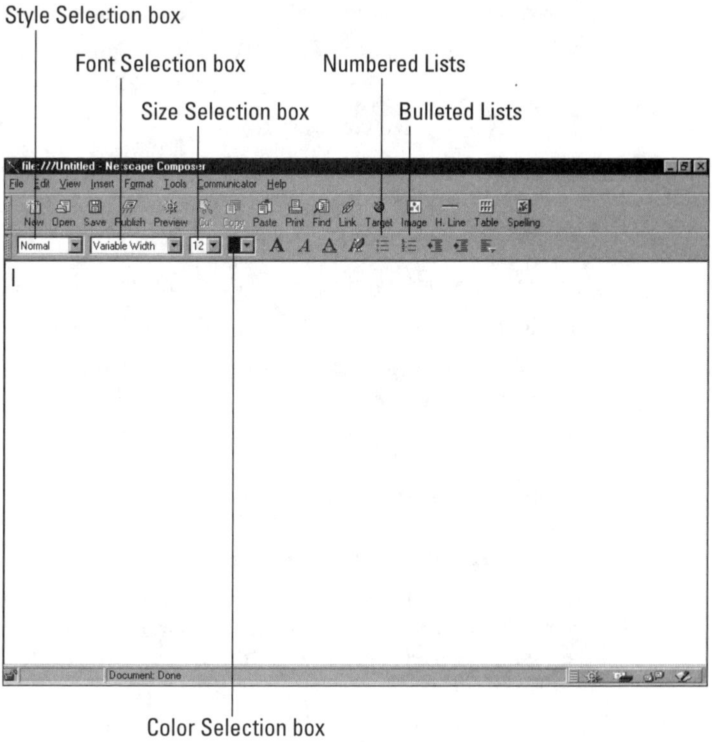

Position your cursor anywhere on the blank page and type away. Composer offers a variety of fonts and colors, and you use them in much the same way you would if you were typing a document in a word processor.

Changing fonts

You can use as many font types within a sentence as you wish. To change a font:

1. Highlight the text for which you want to change fonts.
2. Click on the Font Selection box on the formatting toolbar. A drop-down menu appears listing the available fonts.
3. Click on the font you want to use.

The highlighted text should now have the new font.

Changing the size of text

To change the size of the font within your text:

1. Highlight the text for which you want to change the font size.
2. Click on the Size Selection box on the formatting toolbar. A drop-down menu appears listing the available text sizes.
3. Click on the size you want to use.

The text should now appear in the new size.

Changing the color of text

You can use a variety of colors within your text. To change a color:

1. Highlight the text for which you want to change colors.
2. Click on the Color Selection box on the formatting toolbar. A color palette appears.
3. Click on the color you want to use.

The highlighted text should now have the new color.

Changing the paragraph style

The text within a home page can be categorized into a variety of styles, called *paragraph styles,* depending on what the text looks like. Using a variety of styles within the page makes your page easier to read.

Your page may have many sections, each of which has subsections within it. Typing all your section headings using one style and all your subsection headings in another style gives your page a uniform look, thereby making it easier for a reader to follow the flow of content within the page.

The following paragraph styles are available within Composer, each with its own distinctive look:

- Headings
- Address
- List Item
- Formatted
- Description Title
- Description Text

To apply a style to a piece of text:

1. Highlight the text to which you want to apply the new style.
2. Click on the Style Selection box on the formatting toolbar. A drop-down menu appears listing the available styles.
3. Click on the style you want to use.

The highlighted text should now have the new style.

Creating a bulleted list

To create a bulleted list:

1. Position the cursor in the page where you want the list to begin.
2. Click on the Bullet List button on the formatting toolbar. This displays a bullet at the position where the cursor was, creating the first item of your bulleted list.
3. Start typing your text for that bullet.
4. Press Enter. This creates a bullet on the next line, creating the second item for your bulleted list. Type the text for that bullet.
5. After you create all your bulleted items, press Enter again. This creates a bullet on the next line, as expected. Leave this last bulleted item empty.
6. Click on the Bullet List button on the formatting toolbar. The empty bulleted item at the end of your bulleted list disappears. Your bulleted list is complete.

Creating a numbered list

To create a numbered list:

1. Position the cursor in the page where you want the list to begin.
2. Click on the Numbered List button on the formatting toolbar. A # sign appears where the cursor was.

   Even though you expected to see the number 1 in place of the # sign, you've done nothing wrong. Trust me! The numbers in the numbered list appear just fine when you view the page within a browser.
3. Start typing your text for that numbered item.
4. Press Enter. This puts a # sign on the next line, creating your next item in the numbered list. Type the text for that item.

5. After you create all your numbered items, press Enter again. This puts a # sign on the next line, as expected. Leave this last numbered item empty.

6. Click on the Numbered List button on the formatting toolbar. The last numbered item on the list disappears. Your numbered list is complete.

Adding a link

A *link* on a home page is a word, phrase, or image that you click on from within a browser, to go you to another section within the same page, or to another home page or Web site. For example, your home page may mention your friend Jennifer who has a home page on the Web. You can link the word *Jennifer* in your page to her home page, so that when a reader visits your home page and clicks on *Jennifer,* the reader goes to Jennifer's home page.

Just follow these steps to turn an item on your page into a link:

1. Type the text which you plan to use as the linked word or phrase. Or insert an image if you want to use that as a link.

2. Highlight the item — the text or image — that you want to use as a link and click on the Link button on the Composer toolbar. The Character Properties window appears displaying the Link tab.

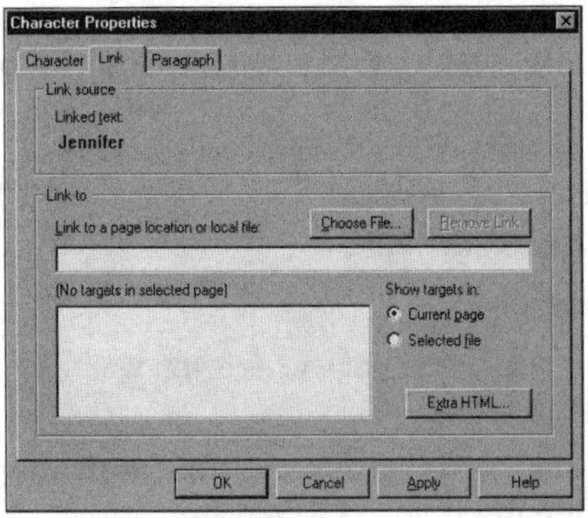

3. In the Link to a page location or local file box, type the URL for the item you wish to link to.

   If the link you're creating goes to a page on another Web site, begin the URL with **http://**. For example, if the link is to `www.coolsite.com`, you should type **http://www. coolsite. com**.

If the link is a *local link* (to a page within the same directory as the page you're creating), just type the name of the file you're linking to. This tells Composer that the linked file is in the same directory as the page you're creating.

4. Click on OK. You return to the Composer screen.

TIP: To confirm that the text or image you just linked to has been linked properly, move the mouse pointer over the link. The URL you linked the text or image to should appear at the bottom of the Composer window in the status bar.

Keeping your links updated

What happens if you change the location of the current page a week from now? The URL will be invalid. You can ask Composer to make sure that your links stay valid. Composer can automatically update the links to reflect the change. Here's how:

1. Choose Edit⇨Preferences. The Preferences window appears.
2. In the Category section, click on the Publishing category listed under Composer to make the Publishing options appear on the right side of the window.

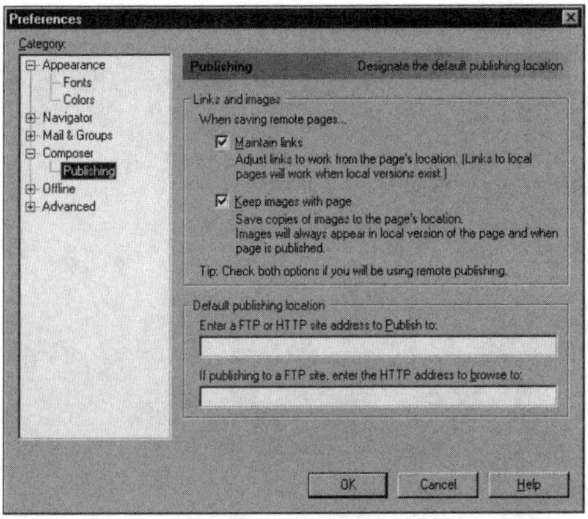
Preferences
Category:
Appearance
Fonts
Colors
Navigator
Mail & Groups
Composer
Publishing
Offline
Advanced
Publishing
Designate the default publishing location
Links and images
When saving remote pages...
Maintain links
Adjust links to work from the page's location. (Links to local pages will work when local versions exist.)
Keep images with page
Save copies of images to the page's location.
Images will always appear in local version of the page and when page is published.
Tip: Check both options if you will be using remote publishing.
Default publishing location
Enter a FTP or HTTP site address to Publish to:
If publishing to a FTP site, enter the HTTP address to browse to:
OK
Cancel
Help

3. Click on the check box next to Maintain links.
4. Click on OK. You return to the Composer screen.

Adding an image

Images on a home page can be either in GIF or JPG format. Technically, Composer also lets you use images in the bitmap (BMP) format file, too, because the program automatically converts the BMP image to JPG format before adding it to the page.

You can add an image to your Composer screen in two ways, depending on the location of the image; the image can either be on another Web site or on your computer.

Here's something you ought to know about using images you find on the Web. If the image was created by someone else, you should request permission from its owner before you use it on your home page. Copyright laws that apply to photographs and images on paper apply to those on the Web, too.

To add an image from another Web site:

1. Drag and drop the image from the home page onto the Composer screen. It's as simple as that. The image should appear on the Composer screen.
2. Right-click on the image on the Composer screen.
3. In the menu that appears, click on Image Properties. Skip down to Step 5 in the next numbered list.

If the image you want to use is on your computer, here's how you insert it in your home page:

1. Position the cursor where you'd like the image to appear.
2. Click on the Image button on the toolbar. The Image Properties window appears.

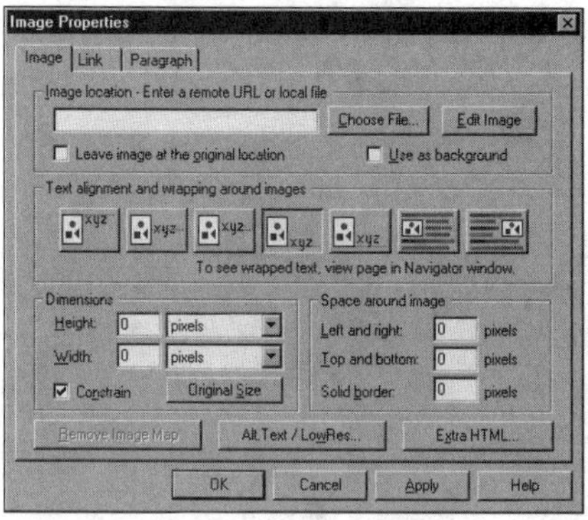

3. Click on Choose File. The Choose Image File window appears.
4. Select an image and click on Save to return to the Image Properties window.

5. If you intend to eventually keep the image in the same directory or folder as your home page, make sure that the check box next to Leave image at the original location does not have a check mark in it. If it does, click on it to remove the check mark.

6. You can specify the image to be either right-aligned or left-aligned to the page margins. You can also specify how you'd like the text around the image aligned. You can have it aligned to top, center, or bottom of the image. To choose an alignment option, click on the button corresponding to your choice in the Text alignment and wrapping around images section.

7. You can specify the dimensions of the image in either the number of pixels or in terms of the relative percentage of the browser window it will occupy when displayed within it. If the dimensions are specified in pixels, then the size of the image when displayed within the browser window stays the same even if the browser window is enlarged or made smaller.

   If the dimensions are specified in terms of the percentage of the browser window it occupies, then the size of the image changes if the size of the browser window displaying it changes. Specify the size of the image within the Height and Width boxes, and also whether you'd like the dimensions to be in pixels or a percentage of the browser window.

8. If you'd like to specify empty space and a border around your image, you can do so in the Space around image section. Empty space around an image makes it stand out, especially if there's text wrapped around it. Specify the amount of empty space in the relevant boxes.

9. Click on Alt.Text/LowRes. The Alternate Image Properties dialog box appears.

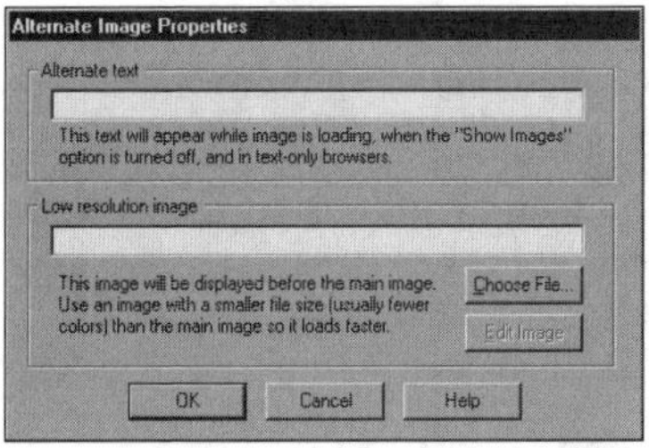
Alternate Image Properties
Alternate text
This text will appear while image is loading, when the "Show Images" option is turned off, and in text-only browsers.
Low resolution image
This image will be displayed before the main image. Use an image with a smaller file size (usually fewer colors) than the main image so it loads faster.
Choose File...
Edit Image
OK
Cancel
Help

Alternate text is text which the browser displays in place of the image when a user elects to turn image display off while viewing your page. The alternate text also appears when the user positions the mouse pointer over the image when the image is displayed. You don't have to specify alternate text if you don't want to; however, using alternate text guarantees that even if image display within a browser is turned off, the user has some clue as to what the image is.

10. Type the alternate text in the Alternate Text box. The text is usually the name of the image file or a brief description of the image.

    If the image you're including in your page is large and has a high resolution, it takes the browser a while to download and display it. While it is being downloaded, you can choose to have a low resolution version of the same image displayed in its place.

    Because the low resolution version is a smaller file, the user has something to look at while the main image — the higher resolution version — is being downloaded in the background. As soon as the higher resolution version has finished downloading, it replaces the low resolution version in the browser.

    The low resolution version should be considerably smaller than the original image, or else it defeats the purpose of asking it to be downloaded. Type the name of this smaller, low resolution image in the Low resolution image box.

11. Click on OK.

12. Click on Apply.

13. Click on Close.

TIP

You can ensure that the image is always located in the same directory as the home page even if you move the home page to another location and forget to move the image file with it. Composer can move the image automatically for you, if you ask it to. Here's how:

1. Choose Edit⇨Preferences. The Preferences window appears.

2. Click on Publishing listed under Composer in the left pane of the window. The Publishing options appear within the right pane of the window.

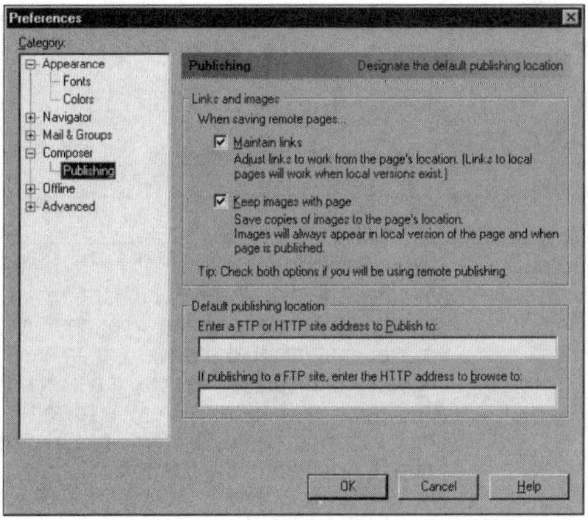

3. Click on the check box next to Keep images with page.

4. Click on OK. You return to the Composer screen.

The images you include in your page will always move with the page when the page is moved to a new folder or directory.

Adding a table

Sometimes you may want to add information to your Web page that looks good in a table, such as your weekly schedule, or perhaps statistical data. Composer makes adding tables to your Web page so easy, you can hardly call it work:

1. Click on the Table button on the toolbar. The New Table Properties dialog box appears.

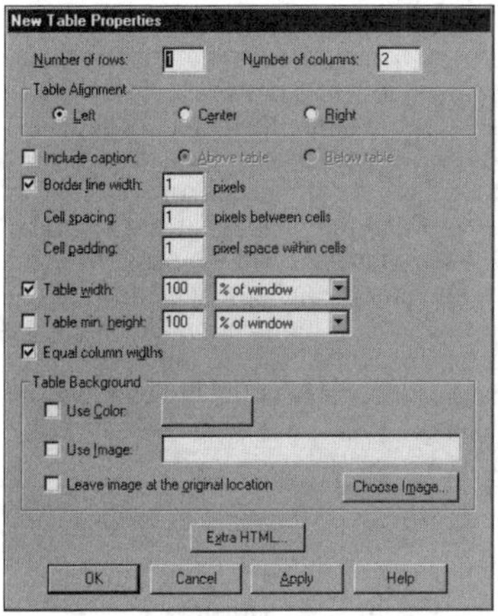

2. Specify the number of rows and columns you want your table to have.

3. Specify the various attributes of the table. You have the following options:

Attribute	*What It Does*
Border line width	Adds a border around the cells and the table, and also specifies the thickness of the borders. You should specify a border during the creation of a table, just so you can confirm that the text within each cell is aligned and displayed exactly the way you want it. After the table has been created to your satisfaction, you can turn off borders, if you don't want to display them, by removing the check mark from the Border line width check box.
Cell spacing	Determines the thickness of the border separating the table's cells
Cell padding	Sets the left, right, top, and bottom margins around the text within each cell
Include caption	Adds a caption above or below the table
Table Alignment	Aligns the table to the left, right, or center of the page
Table Background	Gives you options for adding pretty colors and images
Table width	Determines the width of the table. You can specify the width in either the number of pixels or in terms of the relative percentage of the browser window it will occupy. If the dimensions are specified in pixels, then the width of the table when displayed within the browser window stays the same even if the browser window is enlarged or made smaller. If the dimensions are specified in terms of the percentage of the browser window it occupies, then the width of the table changes if the size of the browser window displaying it changes.
Table min. height	Sets the minimum height of the the table when displayed within a browser window. You can specify the height in either the number of pixels or in terms of the relative percentage of the browser window it will occupy. If the dimensions are specified in pixels, then the height of the table when displayed within the browser window stays the same even if the browser window is enlarged or made smaller. If the dimensions are specified in terms of the percentage of the browser window it occupies, then the height of the table changes if the size of the browser window displaying it changes, but it will never fall below the minimum height you specify.

4. Click on OK.

Your table should appear within the Composer screen.

Adding a table within a table

Yup. You can even have a table within a table. Each cell within a table can have a table of its own. You may do this for further breaking up the contents of a cell. For example, you may want to create a table for your weekly schedule, with one column for each day of the week, and three rows — Morning, Afternoon, Evening — for each day. In any cell, say Monday Afternoon, you can have a table showing the schedule for that afternoon. You may want to do this because the schedule for Monday Afternoon may be the only one in the whole week that needs to be further categorized.

Table in a table

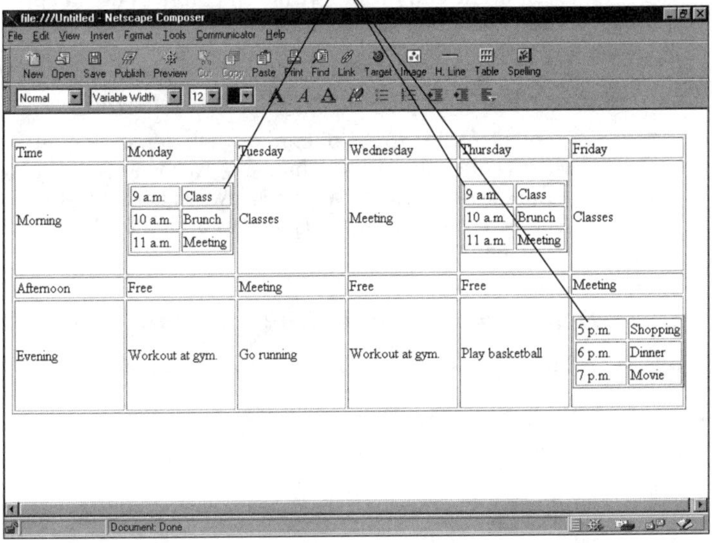

To add a table within a table:

1. Move the cursor to the cell within which you want to create the new table.
2. Click on the Table button on the toolbar. You see the New Table Properties dialog box.
3. Specify the characteristics of the new table.
4. Click on OK. Voilà! The current cell should now have a new table within it.

Editing a table

To change the contents of any cell within the table, position the cursor within the cell and edit its contents.

You can also change the table's characteristics. Say, for example, that you miscalculated the number of rows or columns. You can add or delete rows, columns, and cells from the table. You can also make changes to the attributes of individual rows or cells. For example, you can color cells differently and vary the text alignment from a cell to another. These possibilities are what makes Composer really shine.

Here's how you'd make changes to an existing table:

1. Right-click anywhere within the table. A menu appears displaying several options.
2. Select Insert or Delete, or another option, depending on what you want to do. Yet another menu appears.
3. Select Table, Row, Column, or Cell, depending on what part of the table you want to change. A row is always added below the current row. A column is always added to the right of the current column. A cell is always added to the right of the current cell.

Deleting an image, link, or table

To delete an image or a link from your Web page:

1. Click on the image or link.
2. Press the Delete key.

ZAP! The offensive item disappears with no messy clean up.

To delete a table:

1. Right-click anywhere on the table.
2. Choose Delete⇨Table.

Zap! That table is gone faster than you can blink.

TIP: To delete a table within a table, make sure you right-click only on that table, else you'll delete the parent table and everything within it. Not good.

Creating a Home Page Using a Template

Composer provides six categories of templates covering a variety of styles:

- **Personal/Family:** For creating a fun-filled family home page.
- **Company/Small Business:** For putting your business up on the Web.
- **Department:** For telling the rest of the company everything about your department.
- **Product/Service:** For advertising your product or service.
- **Special Interest Group:** For publicizing the association or special group you belong to.
- **Interesting and Fun:** For extracurricular activities or hobbies or any such fun stuff you may want to tell the world about.

Each category includes sample Web pages. These samples have text and images within them, which you can replace and customize to your liking.

To create a home page using a template:

1. Choose File⇨New⇨Page from Template. The New Page from Template dialog box appears.
2. Click on Netscape Templates. The Netscape Web Page Templates window appears.

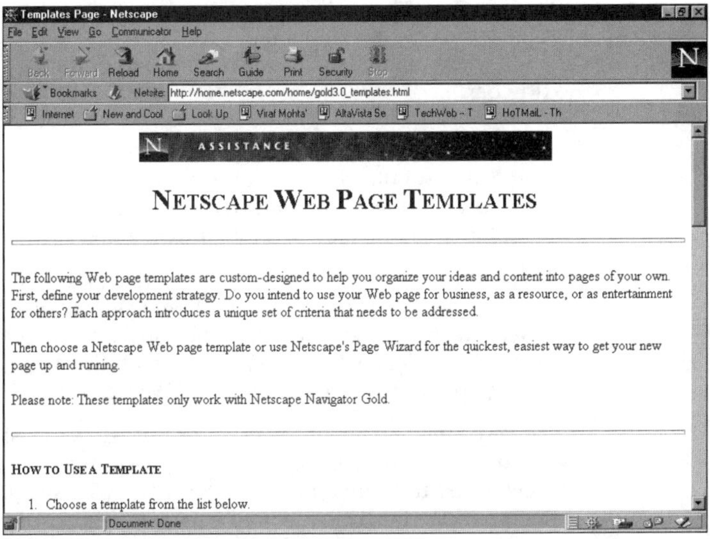
Templates Page - Netscape
File Edit View Go Communicator Help
Back Forward Reload Home Search Guide Print Security Stop
Bookmarks Netsite: http://home.netscape.com/home/gold3.0_templates.html
Internet New and Cool Look Up Viraf Mohta' AltaVista Se TechWeb - T HoTMaiL - Th
ASSISTANCE
NETSCAPE WEB PAGE TEMPLATES
The following Web page templates are custom-designed to help you organize your ideas and content into pages of your own. First, define your development strategy. Do you intend to use your Web page for business, as a resource, or as entertainment for others? Each approach introduces a unique set of criteria that needs to be addressed.
Then choose a Netscape Web page template or use Netscape's Page Wizard for the quickest, easiest way to get your new page up and running.
Please note: These templates only work with Netscape Navigator Gold.
HOW TO USE A TEMPLATE
1. Choose a template from the list below.
Document: Done

3. Scroll down the page until you see a list of templates. Click on the template of your choice.

The selected template opens. For example, if you select the template titled My Home Page, you see the following:

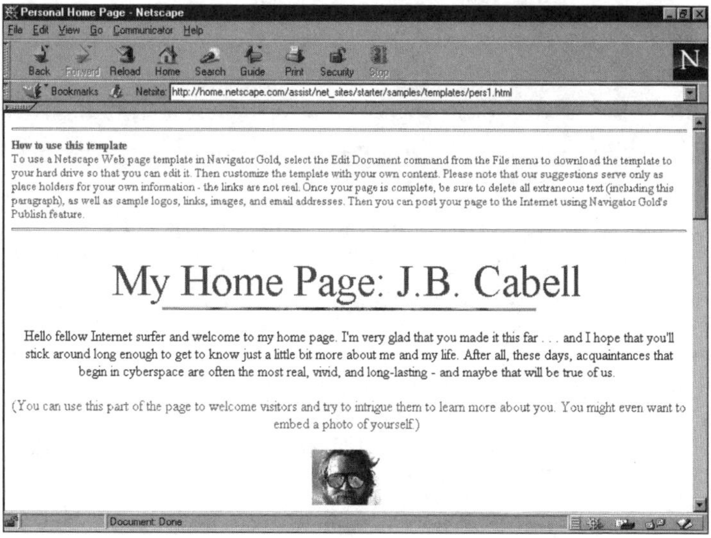
Personal Home Page - Netscape
File Edit View Go Communicator Help
Back Forward Reload Home Search Guide Print Security Stop
Bookmarks Netsite: http://home.netscape.com/assist/net_sites/starter/samples/templates/pers1.html
How to use this template
To use a Netscape Web page template in Navigator Gold, select the Edit Document command from the File menu to download the template to your hard drive so that you can edit it. Then customize the template with your own content. Please note that our suggestions serve only as place holders for your own information - the links are not real. Once your page is complete, be sure to delete all extraneous text (including this paragraph), as well as sample logos, links, images, and email addresses. Then you can post your page to the Internet using Navigator Gold's Publish feature.
My Home Page: J.B. Cabell
Hello fellow Internet surfer and welcome to my home page. I'm very glad that you made it this far . . . and I hope that you'll stick around long enough to get to know just a little bit more about me and my life. After all, these days, acquaintances that begin in cyberspace are often the most real, vivid, and long-lasting - and maybe that will be true of us.
(You can use this part of the page to welcome visitors and try to intrigue them to learn more about you. You might even want to embed a photo of yourself.)
Document: Done

4. Choose File⇨Edit Page.

   Check the title bar. You should see Netscape Composer somewhere on it, usually at the very end of the text on the title bar.

5. Edit the text on the page.

   You can now edit the text on the page like you would a regular word-processing document. Delete the sample text in the template and replace it with your own material.

   To replace a picture with one of your own, right-click on the picture that is already there and then select Image Properties. Select the Image tab and then type the name of your own image in the Image location box. Click on OK. You should now see the picture you selected on the Web page.

   To add a link, highlight the word or phrase you wish to create the link on, right-click on the highlighted text, click on the Link folder tab, and type the URL for the Web site you want to link to in the box titled Link to a page location or local file. For example, to link to the NBC Web site, you would type **http://www.nbc.com.** Click on OK.

   If you are familiar with HTML and would like to add an HTML tag, choose Insert⇨HTML Tag. This brings up the HTML Tag window. Type the HTML tag and click on Verify to confirm that you typed the tag without any errors. Correct errors if any and then click on OK. You won't see the tag you entered in the Composer window. In its place you see a yellow "tag" icon. To modify the HTML code behind the tag, just double-click on the tag icon.

6. Save your Web page by choosing File⇨Save As.

TIP: As you make changes to your page, save it periodically. You don't want to go through the trouble of recovering your page if your system crashes.

Creating a Home Page Using the Wizard

Creating a home page using the Wizard is extremely easy. You follow a question and answer routine, at the end of which your page is ready:

1. Choose File⇨New⇨Page from Wizard. The Netscape Page Wizard appears. Note that there are three frames, or section, on the page, but only one contains text.

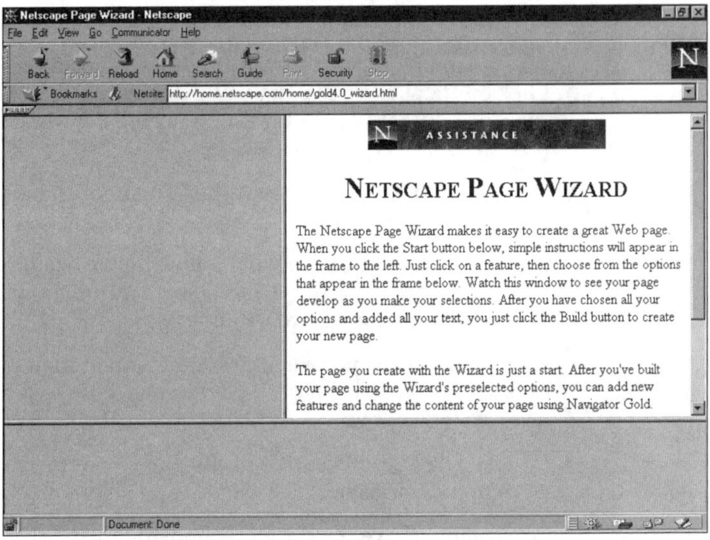
Netscape Page Wizard - Netscape
File Edit View Go Communicator Help
Back Forward Reload Home Search Guide Print Security Stop
Bookmarks Netsite: http://home.netscape.com/home/gold4.0_wizard.html
ASSISTANCE
NETSCAPE PAGE WIZARD
The Netscape Page Wizard makes it easy to create a great Web page. When you click the Start button below, simple instructions will appear in the frame to the left. Just click on a feature, then choose from the options that appear in the frame below. Watch this window to see your page develop as you make your selections. After you have chosen all your options and added all your text, you just click the Build button to create your new page.
The page you create with the Wizard is just a start. After you've built your page using the Wizard's preselected options, you can add new features and change the content of your page using Navigator Gold.
Document: Done

2. Scroll down the frame which contains text and click on START. The next page of the Wizard appears.

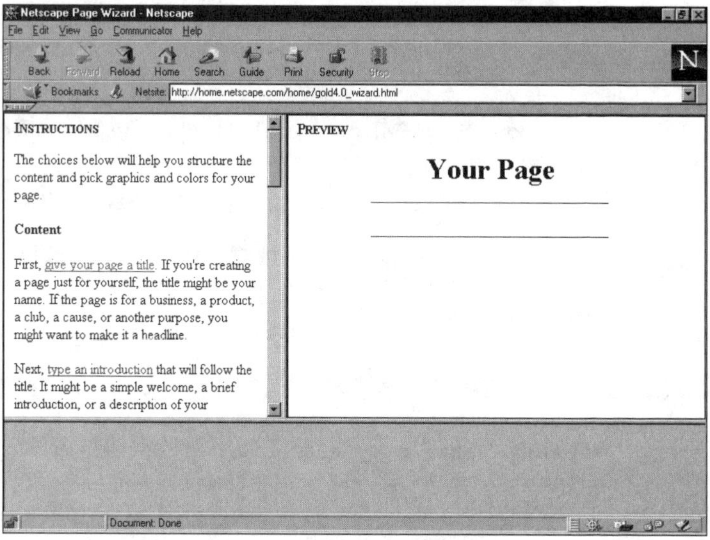
Netscape Page Wizard - Netscape
File Edit View Go Communicator Help
Back Forward Reload Home Search Guide Print Security Stop
Bookmarks Netsite: http://home.netscape.com/home/gold4.0_wizard.html
INSTRUCTIONS
The choices below will help you structure the content and pick graphics and colors for your page.
Content
First, give your page a title. If you're creating a page just for yourself, the title might be your name. If the page is for a business, a product, a club, a cause, or another purpose, you might want to make it a headline.
Next, type an introduction that will follow the title. It might be a simple welcome, a brief introduction, or a description of your
PREVIEW
Your Page
Document: Done

The left frame contains instructions for setting up the page, the right frame shows your page as it's being created, and the bottom frame is where you type the text you want to display on the page, and choose from a variety of other Wizard options such as color and bullet style.

3. Click on the give your page a title link in the left frame. Notice that the contents of the bottom frame change and display a box for you to type your title.

4. Type your title and click on Apply. The right frame of the page now displays your title.

5. Scroll down the left frame and follow the instructions just like you did for creating a title, filling in an introduction, links, and other items as the Wizard prompts you.

6. To save the page, you must first build it and then edit it. Click on Build at the bottom of the left frame. Your page appears in a separate window.

7. Choose File⇨Edit Page to edit the page. Your page appears in Netscape Composer.

8. You can now save the page by choosing File⇨Save.

Editing a Page You're Viewing

You can edit a page you're viewing, directly from within Navigator:

1. Choose File➪Edit Page. Netscape Composer opens and displays the page you were viewing.
2. Add, delete, or change the text, images, and links on the page.

   To add text, position the cursor where you wish to add text and start typing.

   To add an image, position the cursor where you wish to add the image, click on the Insert Image button on the toolbar, type the name of the image file in the Image location box, and click on OK.

   To add a link, first type the text which you wish to link to a Web site. Highlight the text and click on the Link button in the toolbar. Type the URL for the link in Link to box. Make sure that the Current Page radio button is selected in the Show targets in: section. Click on OK.
3. Save page by choosing File➪Save. Give the file a descriptive name — something you'll remember even when awakened in the middle of the night.

TIP

For some reason, people give really cryptic names to their pages. Save yourself headaches and give the file a descriptive name.

Remember: When you edit someone else's home page, you download the page to your machine and edit it there. Although you can edit the page on your own machine, you can't replace the original page in its location with your modified version if you don't have the authority to do so.

Previewing Your Home Page

After you create your home page, you can preview it within Netscape Navigator. All you do is click on the Preview in the Composer toolbar. Navigator opens displaying your page.

If you want to make changes, just return to Composer, make your changes, and click on Preview again. Composer asks if you want to save the changes. You don't have to save the changes if you don't want to.

Publishing Your Home Page

Unless you copy your home page to a Web server, your page can't be seen and appreciated by anybody on the Internet. Unlike your own computer which only you can access, a Web server can be accessed by anybody on the Internet. It's because of this that you can see home pages residing on other people's Web server. Hence, for others to see your home page, you too must publish it on a Web server.

To copy your home page to a Web server, you must have the necessary authorization to do so. You must also know the URL to which you will be copying your files. This information can generally be obtained from your Web Master or System Administrator.

Assuming you have the proper authorization to publish your page, and you know the URL of the location on the server where your files will reside, do the following:

1. Click on the Publish button on the toolbar. The Publish dialog box appears.

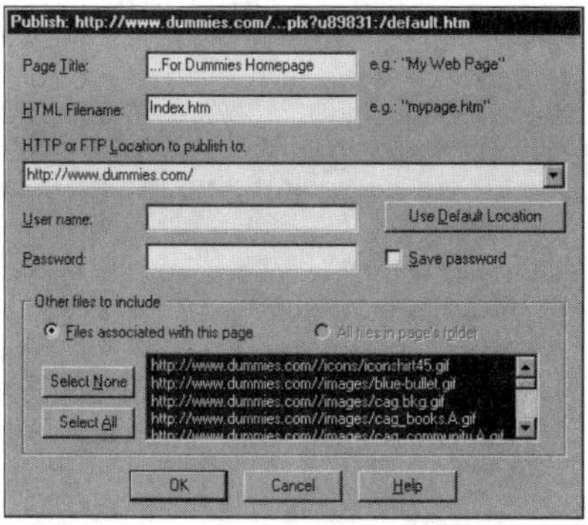

2. If the title in the Page Title box is not descriptive enough for you, you can change it. You don't want your friends calling you up and asking you why you chose `HtmlFile\testdir\Page1.htm` as the title of your page.

   The filename is automatically inserted into the HTML Filename box. Don't change that.

3. In the box titled HTTP or FTP Location to publish to, type the URL of the location where you store your pages.

4. Type your User name and Password that grant you authorization to publish your page on the Web server.

5. If your page contains one or more images, the filenames of each of these images appear in the section titled Other files to include. The Files associated with this page button will be *active,* meaning that all the files listed there are associated with the page being published.

   Because all the files within this box are highlighted, all files will be published or copied to the location you've specified. If you wish to prevent a specific file from being copied to the location, just click on the file name.

6. Click on OK.

Composer publishes your page to the location you specified. Anyone who can access that location from any part of the globe can now view your page. Send an e-mail with your new URL to all your friends and relatives.

Using the Spell Checker

Now you have no excuse for not checking your home pages for spelling mitakes. Sorry, that should be "spelling *mistakes.*" Composer has a built-in spell checker. Like your favorite word processor's spell checker, it too offers suggestions for what it considers to be mistakes, and ignores them, if you ask it to. To begin a spell check, just click on the Spelling button on the toolbar.

Part VI

Netscape Conference

Conference is the most fun option to use within Communicator. Until now, you've probably communicated with your friends on the Web using e-mail or chat. Conference gives you a few more exciting options with which to share information and talk to your friends.

And when I say talk to your friends, I mean that literally. You can actually talk to them like you do when you use the phone. You can even send voice mail like you would on an answering machine. Conference also lets you and a friend browse the Web together, viewing the very same Web sites, one after the other.

Wait, I'm not done yet. Conference has a whiteboard feature that lets you and a friend, located in different places, view and edit a file simultaneously. Any changes you make to the file on the screen show up instantaneously on your friend's screen, and vice versa. You can even transfer files from your computer to your friend's with relative ease. Lastly, Conference also has a built-in chat feature that lets you and a friend chat with each other without having to go to a chat room or fire up special chat software.

In this part . . .

- **Talking with your friends on the Internet**
- **Browsing with other people at the same time**
- **Transferring files**
- **Chatting in real time using text**
- **Editing and viewing images with friends**

Beginning with Conference

Before you get started with Netscape Conference, you need to be aware of the following:

- ✦ Everybody you wish to communicate with using Conference must also have Conference installed on their computers. Installing Communicator automatically installs the Conference option within it, too. But you still need to go through the Conference setup procedure before you can use Conference.
- ✦ You can connect to and communicate with only one user at a time during a Conference session.
- ✦ After you start Communicator, you need to start Conference, too, if you wish to receive calls from other people. You can start it and then leave it active but minimized.

When you start Conference for the first time, Conference automatically starts the Setup Wizard through which you set up various communication options. During this setup procedure, which should take no more than five or ten minutes, the program asks you about a number of things, such as the speed of your modem and the type of sound card you use.

The wizard is smart enough — that's why it's called a wizard — to detect the right answers to most of the questions it asks you. However, you can always change the suggestions it makes during the setup, or at a later date, if you realize the options you set aren't optimal.

If you wish to change the setup options at a later date, choose Help➪Setup Wizard from within the Conference window.

Here's the first of the many windows you see during the setup process.

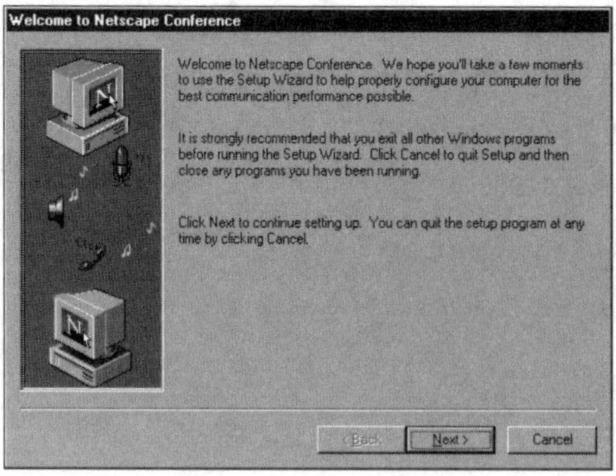
Welcome to Netscape Conference
Welcome to Netscape Conference. We hope you'll take a few moments to use the Setup Wizard to help properly configure your computer for the best communication performance possible.
It is strongly recommended that you exit all other Windows programs before running the Setup Wizard. Click Cancel to quit Setup and then close any programs you have been running.
Click Next to continue setting up. You can quit the setup program at any time by clicking Cancel.
< Back
Next >
Cancel

Click on Next. Answer the questions on the following screens, clicking on Next on each screen to proceed to the next screen. You can revise your answers on any screen at any time by clicking on the Back button. When you get to the last screen, you see the Finish button. Click on Finish to complete the setup process. To exit from the setup process at any time, click on Cancel.

Browsing Together

Collaborative browsing lets you and a friend go on a Web cruise together. In Conference, you get on a call with a friend and the two of you can visit the same Web sites together. What you see, your friend sees, too. When you jump to a different site, so does your friend.

The business applications of collaborative browsing go without saying. Imagine how impressed your boss will be when you lead your clients in another city around your company's Web site. Better start planning what you'll do with that bonus.

Cruising the Web together

To lead a friend on a Web cruise, the two of you need to be connected on a Conference call (***see also*** "Making a Phone Call" in this part). Then follow these steps to have the time of your life:

1. Click on the Collaborative Browsing button on the Conference toolbar. The Collaborative Browsing window appears.

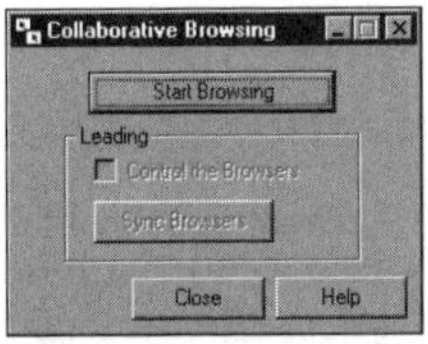

2. Click on Start Browsing. Navigator opens and sends an invitation to your friend to start browsing.

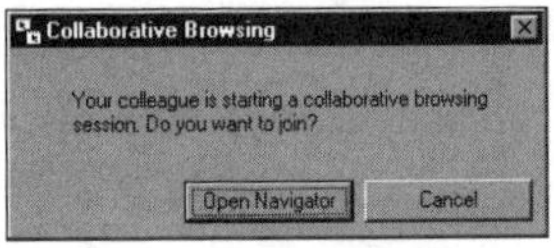

Of course, if your friend is the leader, then you are the lucky recipient of this message.

Accepting the invitation launches Navigator. Rejecting the invitation sends a message to the partner who suggested the collaborative browsing.

After the browsers at both ends are up and running, you can start browsing. Wherever you — the leader — go, your friend's browser goes, too.

3. To end a collaborative browsing session, the leader should return to the Collaborative Browsing window and click on Stop Browsing. Your friend gets the following message:

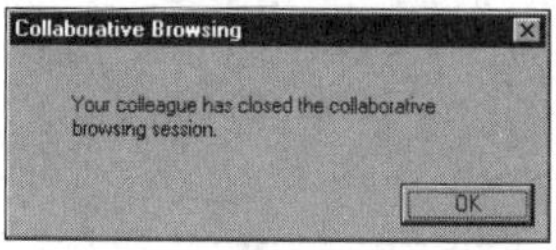

4. Your friend should then return to the Conference window and choose Communicator⇨Collaborative Browsing. The Collaborative Browsing window appears.

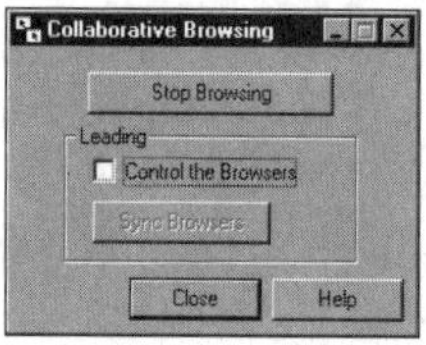

5. Click on Stop Browsing.

Getting the browsers in sync

During a collaborative browsing session, you can make sure that your friend, the one who's following you on your Web cruise, is always viewing the same sites that you are. She may have decided to wander off on her own and may send you an e-mail message saying she did and that she'd like to come back to the session. If you're feeling gracious, you can let her back in and bring both your browsers back in sync with the click of a button. Here's how:

1. Return to the Collaborative Browsing window.
2. Click on Sync Browsers. Both browsers should display the same sites again.

TIP

Only the leader has the option to sync browsers.

Chatting

The chat option within Conference lets you and a friend converse with each other by sending typed messages. This is not the same as e-mail. Chatting in Conference differs from e-mail in that:

- ✦ **Chat happens in real time:** When you send e-mail, you experience a time lag betweeen the time you send the message and the time your friend receives the message. When you use chat, this time lag is nonexistent. What you type immediately appears on your friend's computer screen, and what your friend types immediately appears on yours.
- ✦ **Chat is more spontaneous:** People get more off-the-cuff when chatting than they do in e-mail. You can really think over what you want to say in an e-mail, but while chatting on Conference, unless you have a very patient friend, you don't have too much time to think about your responses.
- ✦ **Chat is more fun:** You get the latest news faster. What could be better than that?

While chatting in Conference, your computer screen appears split into two windows. You type your messages in the lower window, called the Personal Note Pad. The upper window shows the text of the conversation, including what you send as well as what you receive.

Starting up a chat

Before you start a chat session with someone, you need to start a Conference session with that person (***see also*** "Making a Phone Call" in this part). After Conference establishes a connection, you can start chatting. Here's how you go about doing it:

1. Click on the Chat button on the Conference menu bar. The Conference Text Chat window appears. Notice that the cursor is positioned in the lower half of the window.

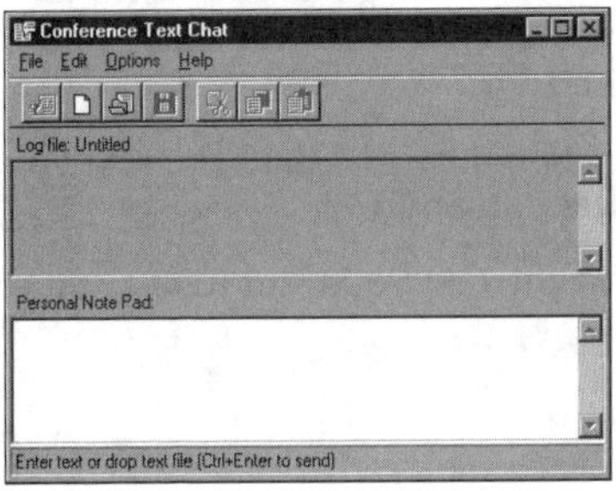

2. Type your message in the lower window, called the Personal Note Pad, and press Ctrl+Enter to send it.

   Your message should appear in the upper window, titled Log File. Replies from the other person also show up in the upper window.

   Your messages have `local user>` before them. Your friend's messages have `remote user>` before them.

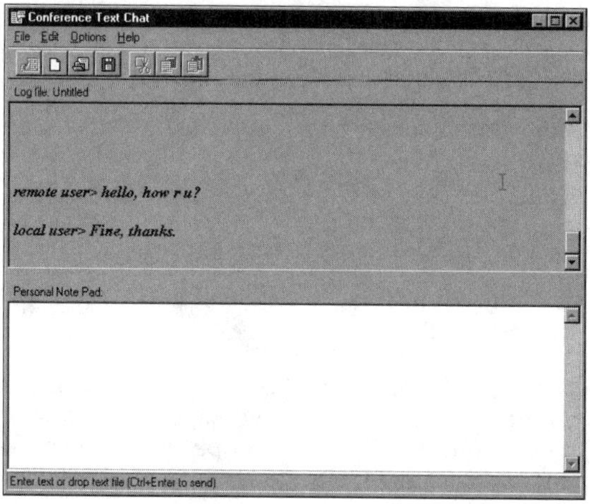

3. To end the chat session, choose File⇨Close.

Editing options during a chat session

Conference offers all kinds of editing options that can help make your chat session more efficient and fun.

You can use "cut-n-paste" options in Conference to add pre-prepared text to your messages. You can also use these options to preserve portions of your text:

- ✦ To paste text from the clipboard into the chat window, position the cursor where you want the text to be pasted and click on the Paste button.
- ✦ To copy text to the clipboard, highlight the text you want to copy and click on the Copy button.
- ✦ To cut text, highlight the text you want to cut and click on the Cut button.

You can use a variety of fonts, font styles, and font sizes when composing your messages in a chat session. To do so:

1. Choose Options⇨Font. The Font dialog box appears.
2. Choose a font, font style, and size from the relevant menus.
3. After you finish editing the font, click on OK.

Your choice of fonts, font styles, and colors appear on your screen only. They don't appear on the screen of the friend you're conducting the chat session with. The fonts on her screen are the ones she chooses to use.

Inserting a file into your chat

When your boss asks for your daily status report during your chat, you can send it to him by placing the file directly into the Personal Note Pad as part of your chat. Conference inserts the file within Personal Note Pad window, and the file shows up as if you had typed the whole report into the chat session.

WARNING!

You can insert only text files in a chat session. You can't insert images or multimedia files. In addition, you should only insert small text files. Big text files containing pages and pages of text are cumbersome to read within the chat window.

To insert a text file:

1. In your Personal Note Pad window, position the cursor where you want to insert the file.
2. Click on the Include button. The Include File Into Pad window appears.
3. Select the file you want to insert.
4. Click on Open. The file appears in your Personal Note Pad window.
5. Click on Send or press CTRL+Enter to send the message with the inserted file.

The file should appear in the Log File window above the Personal Note Pad window.

Saving your chat session text to a file

You can maintain a log of the conversation during a chat session, if you think you may need to refer to it later. The Log File window contains a log of your conversation during the chat session. You can save the contents of the Log File window to a file on your computer at any time during the chat session. You can then periodically update the saved log file as your chat session progresses.

To create a log file and save the contents of your chat session within it:

1. Choose File⇨Save. The Save Log File window appears where you can specify a name and location for the file.
2. Type a filename.
3. Click on Save.

TIP

Don't forget to perodically save the chat session to the log file by clicking on Save. Otherwise, the log file will contain only the portion of the chat session that was saved the last time.

Toolbar

The Chat toolbar shown below allows one-click access to several tasks within a chat session:

Toolbar Button	What It Does
	Sends the message you just typed
	Starts a new log file
	Inserts a text file into your message
	Saves a log of the chat session to a file
	Cuts the selected text and places it on the Clipboard
	Copies the text onto the Clipboard
	Pastes the contents of the Clipboard into the message

Editing Graphics with the Whiteboard

The whiteboard is a really neat tool that lets you and a friend get on a Conference call and then look at and edit a graphics file together.

After you establish a Conference call with your friend (***see also*** "Making a Phone Call" in this part), follow these steps to start editing a graphics file:

1. Click on the Whiteboard button on the Conference toolbar. The Conference Whiteboard window opens on both your screen and your friend's screen at the same time.

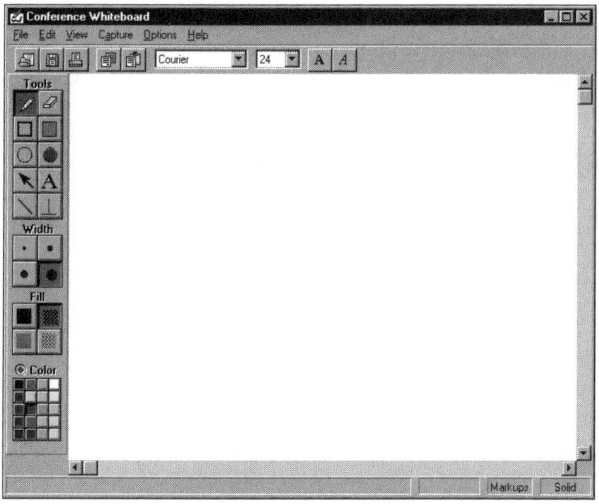

2. Click on the Open button on the Whiteboard toolbar to select the file you want to view. The Open dialog box appears.

3. Select the graphics file you want to work on and click on Open. The Whiteboard window appears with a dotted square within it. The square is attached to your mouse pointer. As you move the mouse pointer, the square moves, too.

4. Position the square where you want to place the image on the Whiteboard screen and click. The image should now appear in the Whiteboard window on your screen as well your friend's.

5. Edit the image using the Toolbox. Changes you make to the image immediately show up on your friend's screen and vice versa.

6. To end the Whiteboard session, choose File⇨Close.

You can also use the whiteboard to edit graphics when you are not on a Conference call.

Synchronizing whiteboards

You and the person you're conferencing with both have the ability to make changes to an image on the whiteboard. The two screens can be out of sync if the two of you are at far corners of the globe and either your Internet connection or your friend's is particularly slow during the session.

A slow connection may not transmit the changes you make on your whiteboard to your friend's whiteboard immediately. If you feel this is the case, and you're not sure what the whiteboard on your friend's computer shows, you can synchronize that whiteboard with yours. This way you can be sure that the whiteboard at the other end looks exactly the same as yours, with exactly the same edits and markups. To synchronize the other whiteboard's images yours, choose Edit⇨Synchronize Page.

Saving a whiteboard image

After you make changes to an image during a Conference call, you can save the revised image. To save the image:

1. Click on the Save button on the Whiteboard toolbar. The Save As window appears.
2. Type a name for the revised image and click on Save.

Your image is saved. You can continue working on the whiteboard and keep saving periodically.

Undoing your edits

If you'd like to erase all changes you make to an image and return it to its original state, you can do so by choosing Edit⇨ Clear Markups.

WARNING! Just keep in mind that choosing Edit⇨Clear Markups erases all changes you've made to the image, not just the last one.

If you'd like to erase individual changes you've made to an image:

1. Choose Options⇨Erase Markups. (This also ensures that you only erase markups you've made to the image, and not the image itself.) The Image/Markups indicator at the lower-right corner of the whiteboard displays the edit option you have selected.
2. Choose the width of the eraser from one of the four sizes available in the Width section of the Tools toolbox. The wider the eraser, the larger the area of the markup and its surrounding area that gets erased.
3. Click on the Eraser icon in the toolbox. The mouse pointer changes to an eraser.
4. Hold the left mouse button down and drag the eraser over the area you want to erase.

The following figure shows the mouse pointer as an eraser, and an image being erased with it.

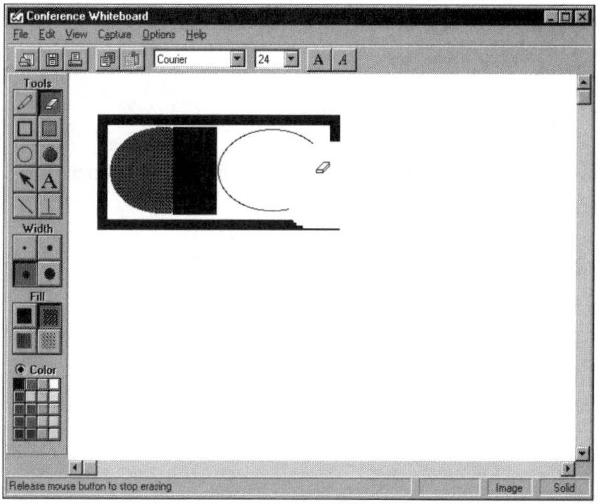

Using the Whiteboard toolbar and Toolbox

The Whiteboard window has two sets of buttons on it. One is the toolbar across the top, right under the menu bar. The other is down the left edge of the window, and is called the Toolbox.

Toolbar Button	What It Does
	Opens a file to bring into the whiteboard
	Saves the currently displayed file to disk
	Prints the currently displayed file
	Allows you to mark a portion of the image and copy it to the Clipboard
	Allows you to paste the contents of the Clipboard on the whiteboard
	Lets you choose a font
	Lets you specify a font size
	Bolds text
	Italicizes text

The Toolbox gives you various options to create and edit markups to an image.

Toolbox Button	*What It Does*
	Draws just like you would with a pencil
	Erases items on the whiteboard
	Adds an empty rectangle
	Adds a filled rectangle
	Adds an empty circle
	Adds a filled circle
	Places an arrow on the whiteboard
	Lets you add text
	Draws diagonal lines
	Draws vertical or horizontal lines
	Determines the width of lines and the eraser
	Selects the pattern for filling circles and rectangles
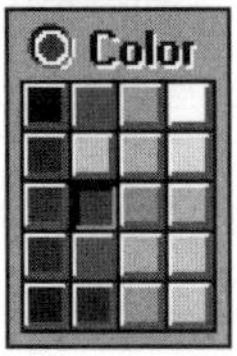	Selects a color for drawing on the whiteboard.

Exchanging Files

The most common way to send files to anyone is by attaching them to an e-mail message. However, if you are already on a Conference call, you may find it more efficient to send your friend a file directly from Conference, rather than switching over to Messenger to attach a file to an e-mail. Likewise, your friend can also send you a file.

Exchanging files is different from inserting a file during a chat session. During a chat session, you're limited to sending text files only. But exchanging files allows you to send any kind of file your little heart desires. Besides, the contents of a text file inserted in a chat session show up as a message typed by you within the Personal Note Pad window. Contents of a file sent from within the Exchanging Files window aren't displayed anywhere within it.

Conference lets you send any type of file you wish. If your file is very large, Conference even compresses your file for you before sending it. What a great program!

Before you can send files to or receive files from anyone, you need to start a Conference session with that person (***see also*** "Making a Phone Call" in this part).

Sending a file

To get in on the wonderful world of sending files:

1. Click on the File Exchange button in the Conference window. The Conference File Exchange window appears.

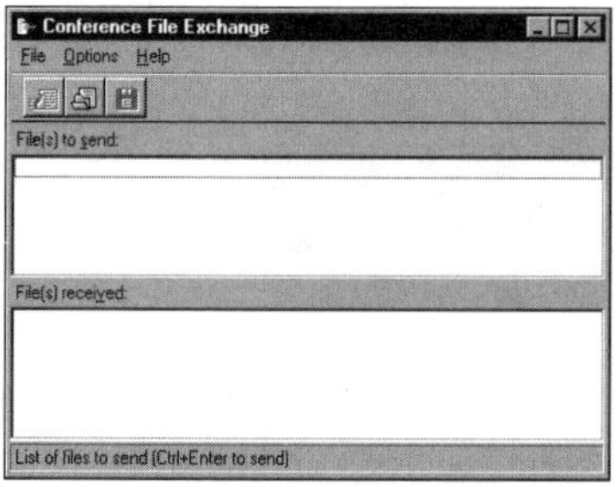

2. Choose Options and then choose one of the following:

   - **ASCII:** Select this option if you're sending a plain text file, which is a file without any formatting like special fonts, bold, italics, colors, or tables, and which hasn't been saved in a special word-processing format such as Microsoft Word or WordPerfect.

- **Binary:** Select this option if the file you're sending is anything other than a plain text file, such as image files, sound files, spreadsheets, data base files, and even text files saved in a special word processor such as Microsoft Word or WordPerfect.

If you want to send more than one file, all the files should be of the same type, either ASCII or Binary. If you have to send both types of files, then send one type of file first and then repeat the send procedure to send the other type of file. The two types of files can't be sent together.

3. If you want to compress a large file before sending it, choose Options⇨Compress. Selecting Compression automatically compresses all files before sending them.

   You don't need to do any extra work in compressing them. File Exchange takes care of that for you. At the receiving end, File Exchange again decompresses the compressed files. No extra work there, either.

   Although compressing and decompressing files adds a couple extra steps in the file transmission process, it speeds up the transmission of files. I recommend that you compress all files before sending them, especially if you're sending more than one file at a time.

4. Click the Open button. The Add File to Send List window appears.

5. Select the file yow7gant to send. Remember to add only that kind of file — either ASCII only or Binary only — depending on the type of file you selected earlier. The file should now appear in the File(s) to send area of the Conference File Exchange window.

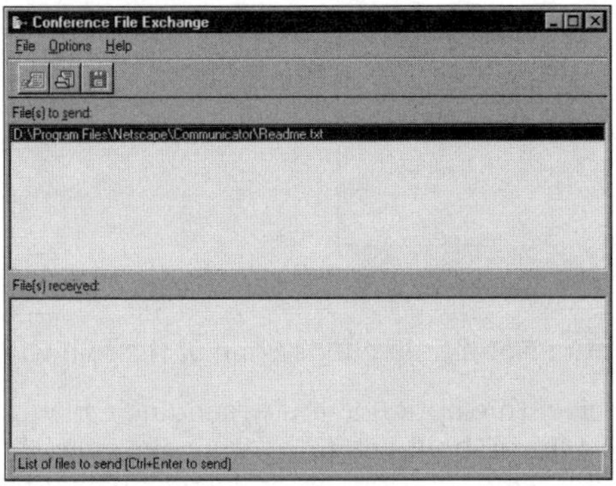

6. Repeat Steps 1 through 5 to select as many files as you want (you can send more than one file at a time).

7. To send just one file listed in the File(s) to send window, highlight only that file and click on Send. To send more than one file at a time, highlight all files you wish to send and click on Send.

Receiving a file

To receive files from someone, you have to be on a call within Conference with that person. When you receive a file from the person you're on Conference with, the File Exchange window automatically pops up on your screen, listing the received file in the File(s) received portion of the window.

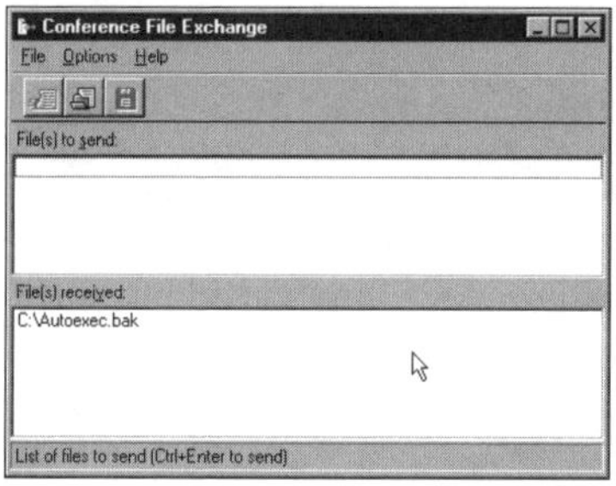

Before you can read a received file, you first need to save it to your hard drive:

1. Click on the filename to select it.

2. Click on Save button on the toolbar. The Save Received File window appears.

3. Type a name for the file and select a location for it, too. Then click on Save.

Conference saves the file to the specified location, and the file disappears from the File(s) received window.

Toolbar

The File Exchange toolbar consists of only three buttons:

Toolbar Button	What It Does
	Sends the selected files in the File(s) to send window
	Adds a file to the Send list
	Saves the selected file in the File(s) received window

Making a Phone Call

How often have you gotten your long distance phone bill and gone through the roof seeing what you owed? Yup, it happens to the best of us. Thankfully, Conference offers audio options that let you make phone calls to friends on the Web. Unfortunately, you can talk to only one person at a time. But Conference calls cost you nothing except the cost of the local phone call you make to your ISP to get on the Web.

To make a Conference call, your computer must sport the following hardware:

- A sound card
- A microcophone
- Speakers

The quality of your Conference call can be influenced by any and all of the following factors:

- The speed of your modem and your computer
- The Silence Sensor setting on both computers ***(see also*** "Adjusting the microphone and speaker audio levels")
- The traffic on the Internet

Sometimes the audio coming out of your speakers may sound choppy and distorted. Assuming that you have set up the options within Conference properly, you can't do much to improve the quality of the sound, because you have no control over the amount of traffic on the Internet.

Because all you need to call someone is his or her e-mail address, Conference makes it easy for you to call anybody. You call the person using the same address you use for sending e-mail messages to that person from within Messenger.

To call someone who isn't listed in your Address Book:

1. Type the person's e-mail address in the E-mail address box.
2. Click on Dial.

To call someone who's listed in your Address Book, follow these steps:

1. Click on the Address Book button within your Conference window. The Address Book window appears.

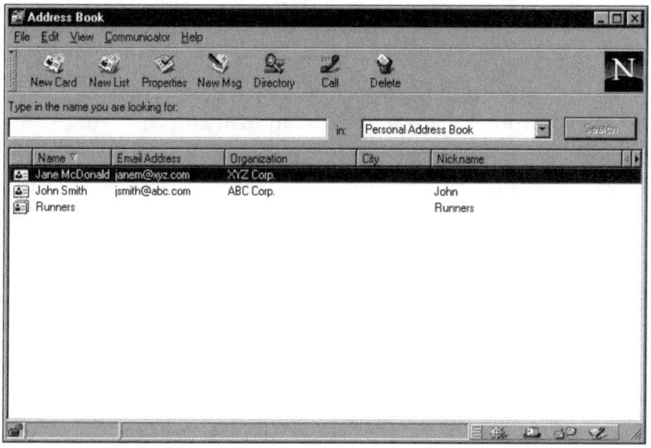

2. Click on the name of the person you want to call and then click on the Call button on the toolbar.

   Conference dials the e-mail address of the person. The Pending Invitation dialog box appears displaying the status of your call.

   If the person you dialed is connected to the Internet and accepts your invitation, Conference establishes a connection. You can tell that a connection has been made because the Dial button within your Conference window now displays Hang Up instead of Dial.

3. Start speaking into your computer's microphone. You should also hear your friend's voice through your computer's speakers.

   If that person doesn't have Communicator up and running on his or her computer or isn't connected to the Internet or company intranet, you see the Voice Mail dialog box telling you that the person is not available and asking you if you'd like to leave a message.

If you'd like to leave a voice mail message, click on Yes. The voice recorder opens, allowing you to record an audio message and send it. (***See also*** "Recording a voice message to send via e-mail.")

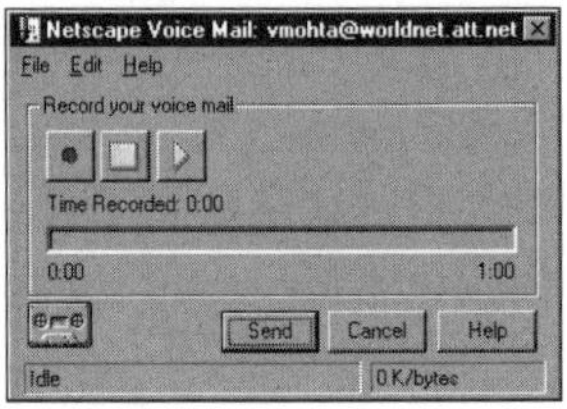

If you don't want to send a voice mail message, click on No.

If the person is connected to the Internet or the intranet, and either doesn't answer your invitation, or refuses your invitation to talk, the Pending Invitation dialog box appears giving you the bad news. Don't be disheartened. Just click on OK to try another friend.

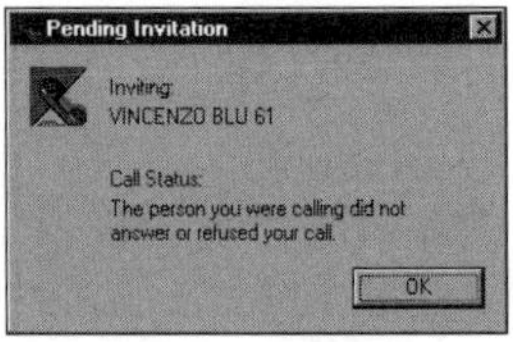

Calling a person listed in the Web Phonebook

None of your friends have Conference, and you're aching to talk to someone who does. How do you go about finding someone who uses Conference? You use the Web Phonebook, which lists all registered Conference users. At any given time, you can get a list of all Conference users who are currently connected to the Web.

Here's how you go about contacting another Conference user:

1. Click on the Web Phonebook button within the Conference window. The Netscape Conference Directory Web site appears, listing all Conference users currently connected to the Web.

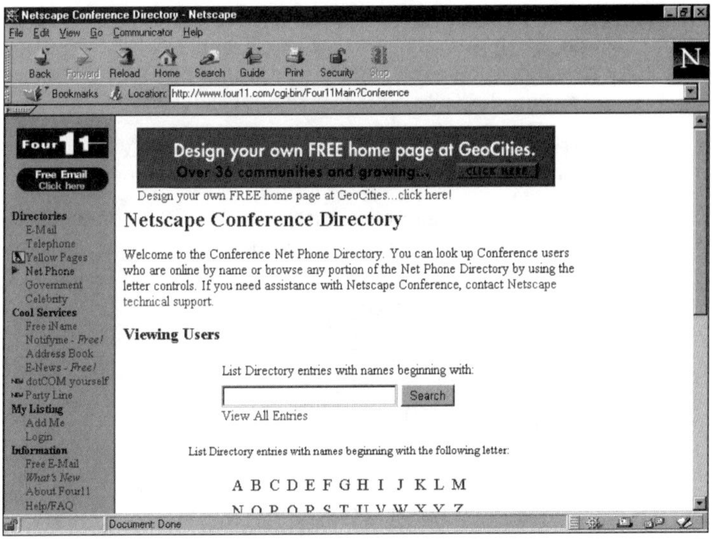

2. Scroll down the page and click on a letter from the alphabet listing for directory entries of all current users whose names begin with that letter.

3. If there are current users of Conference whose names begin with that letter, Conference tells you who they are, with their e-mail adresses.

4. To call a person on the list, click on the Call with Netscape Conference link right under the person's name. Conference calls the person in an attempt to make a connection. You see the Pending Invitation dialog box as Conference dials. If the person doesn't answer your call or turns down your request for talking, you see a message in the Pending Invitation window stating this.

5. Click on OK to return to the Conference window and try another user.

Recording a voice message to send via e-mail

You can send a recorded message via e-mail from within Conference. Conference offers a built-in recorder that lets you record the message.

WARNING! Your voice message can be no more than four minutes long. After four minutes, the recorder automatically stops recording. A timer tells you how much time you have left as you record your message, just in case you are the verbose type.

If you try to call a friend who isn't available, Confererence gives you the option of sending a voice-mail. If you accept the offer of sending a voice-mail message, Conference automatically activates the recorder to let you record a message.

If you want to record a message for a friend without first trying to establish a Conference call, follow these steps:

1. Choose Communicator⇨Voice Mail. The Recipient email address needed window appears.

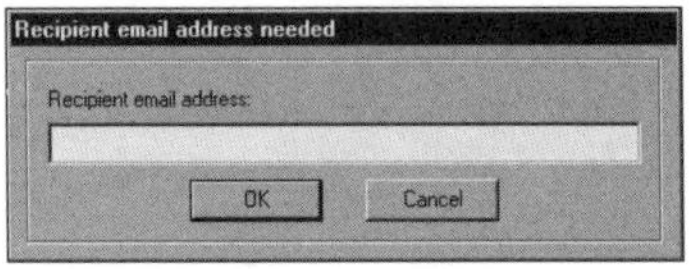

2. Type the e-mail address of the person you're calling in the Recipient email address box.
3. Click on OK. The Netscape Voice Mail window appears, displaying the recorder.

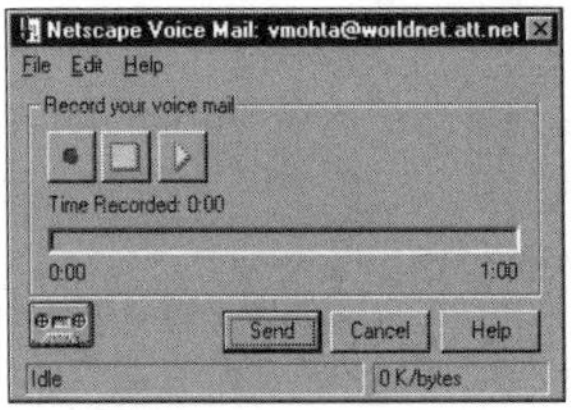

4. Click on the record button, the one with the red dot on it, to start recording. Speak clearly into your microphone.
5. After you finish your message, click on the Stop button, the one with the white square on it.
6. Click on the Play button, the one with the triangle on it, to listen to the recorded message.

   If you're not satisfied with the message, you can re-record it by clicking on the record button again. The Netscape Voice Mail dialog box appears alerting you that you have already recorded a message, and if you'd like to record a new message, you need to delete the current one. Click on Yes and start recording.
7. Click on Send to send your message. The Message Composition window appears. Notice that the To box contains the recipient's e-mail address, and the text area of the message has the Netscape Voice Mail icon in it.

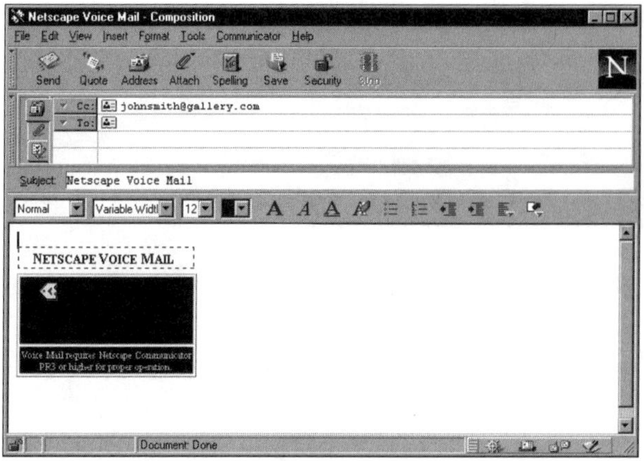

8. Type a message in the text portion of the Message Composition window.

9. Click on Send. Your voice mail is on its way.

TIP

Conference sets the maximum length of your messages at four minutes. If you want your messages to always be shorter than that, you can set the maximum number of minutes beyond which you'd like the recorder to automatically stop recording. Here's how:

1. Choose Edit⇨Preferences. The Preferences window appears.

2. In the Maximum Length (minutes) box, type the number of minutes you want your message to be. Remember, four minutes is the maximum, and you must stipulate whole numbers.

Adding an e-mail address to Speed Dial

Conference has a built-in Speed Dial function that lets you store e-mail addresses of people you call frequently. You can store up to six addresses. Here's how:

1. Click on Show Speed Dial button within the Conference window. It's a tiny little button right under the Web Phonebook button. Six buttons, labeled Speed Dial 1 through Speed Dial 6, appear right under that button.

2. Click on any button. You now see the Speed Dial Edit dialog box.

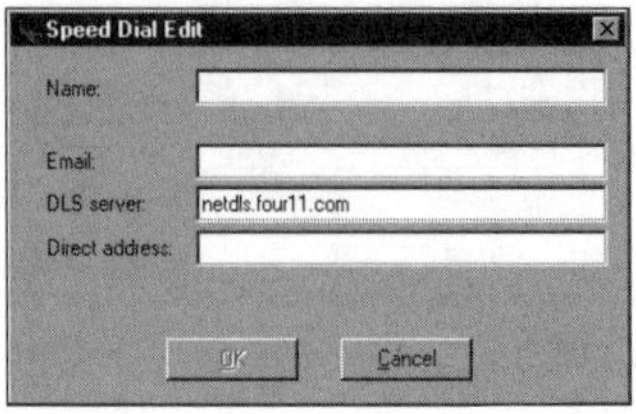

3. Enter the person's name and the e-mail address in the relevant boxes.

4. Click on OK. Conference now displays the person's name on the Speed Dial button.

To call a person assigned to a Speed Dial button, just click on the button with the person's name on it.

Setting call receive options

When someone calls you within Conference, you can tell Conference how to respond by choosing one of the three following options:

- **Choose Call⇨Auto Answer:** Conference automatically answers the call and establishes an audio connection with the caller.
- **Choose Call⇨Always Prompt:** Conference prompts you to either accept or refuse the call.
- **Choose Call⇨Do Not Answer:** Conference automatically refuses the call.

Adjusting the microphone and speaker audio levels

Improper audio settings for your microphone are are the primary cause of poor voice transmission and recording within Conference. You want to make sure that your voice is the only sound that gets transmitted or recorded.

By adjusting the Silence Sensor on the recorder properly, you can ensure that recording or transmisson begins only when you speak. Although you may have set this within the Setup Wizard when you started Conference for the very first time, you can adjust these settings at any time thereafter.

Here's how you adjust the recording or transmission setting:

1. Turn on your microphone if it has an on/off switch.

2. Click on the microphone icon within the Conference window. Speak into your microphone normally. You see a color bar in the recording level meter, indicating the audio level.

   The bar has a green portion on the left, turning into a red one, followed by a bright red one. The bright red one shows up only if you speak loudly. The light red bar indicates the level at which your voice is recognized by the microphone. The green bar indicates unnecessary background noise which shouldn't be transmitted or recorded.

3. Continue speaking and drag the Silence Sensor, which is the blue tab in the recording level meter, to the right, so that it is positioned right where the green bars end and the light red ones begin.

4. The Sensitivity Level indicator under the recording level indicator is the volume control for the sound transmit. You need to adjust this volume according to what the person at the other end of your call can or can not hear. But for the time being, drag the indicator to the center of the level.

5. The Speaker level indicator adjusts the volume of the sound you hear on your speaker. You can adjust it properly only when you've made a phone connection and are talking to someone. For now, drag the indicator to the center of the level.

Part VIII

Netscape Calendar

Calendar, which is only available in the Professional version of Communicator, is a time scheduling program. With it you can schedule appointments, jot down tasks, mark important dates, and set reminders to nudge you about that anniversary next week. It's a wonderful tool which takes over the drudgery of remembering appointments and errands.

If you use Calendar on your company network or intranet, you can coordinate meetings and schedules with your colleagues. Even if you aren't connected to such a network, you can still use Calendar to keep things on track.

In this part . . .

- **Getting organized**
- **Staying on schedule**
- **Setting reminders about appointments**
- **Keeping track of tasks**

Beginning Your Day with Calendar

To start Calendar:

1. Choose Communicator⇨Calendar. The Netscape Calendar Sign-In dialog box appears.

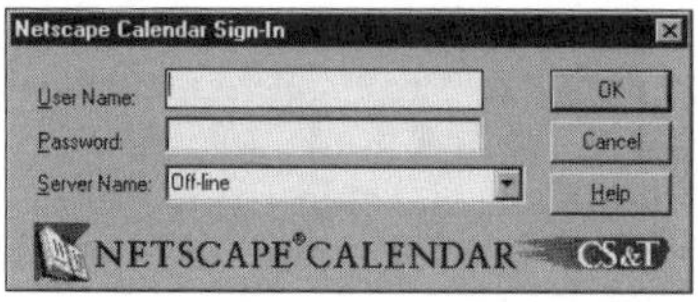

2. Type your name and password. This is the name and password which the network identifies you by. If you're not connected to a network, you see Off-line in the Server Name box.

3. Click on OK. The Calendar window appears showing the current day's appointments.

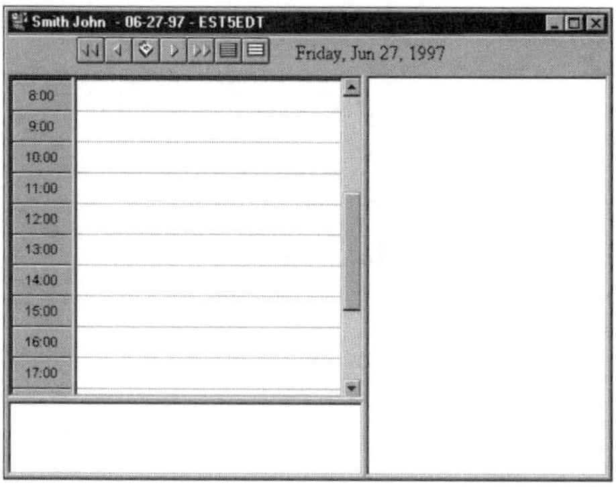

Making Entries in Your Calendar

Your appointments, meetings, reminders, in short, all entries you make to your Calendar, form your Agenda. If you need to keep track of something, you can enter it into Calendar.

Creating an Agenda entry

1. Within the Day Agenda view, check the date at the top of the window. If it's not the date for which you want to schedule the

event, click on the Calendar button in the Date Control bar and pick a date from the calendar that appears.

The chosen date's agenda appears.

2. Click on the time slot when you want to schedule your entry or event to highlight it.

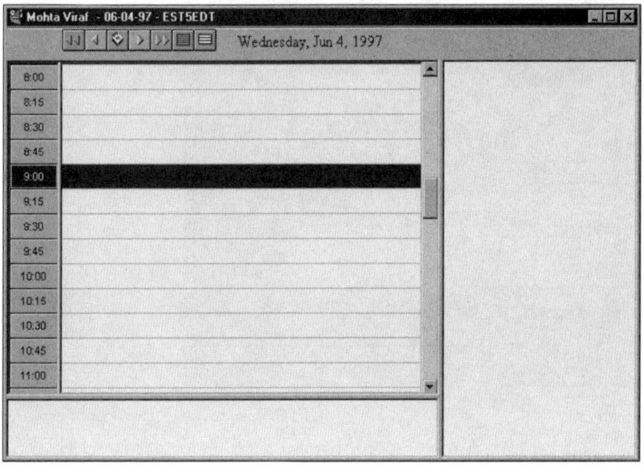

3. Type a description for the event and press Enter. Calendar enters your event for that time slot.

Deleting an Agenda entry

Simply deleting the text of the entry by using the Del key only ends up creating an empty entry which still resides in the Agenda. To delete the entry completely from the Agenda:

1. Click on the entry. This highlights the entry and positions the cursor in the entry field.
2. Choose Edit⇨Delete Entry. A dialog box appears asking if you really want to delete the entry. Notice that the entry in question also appears in the dialog box.

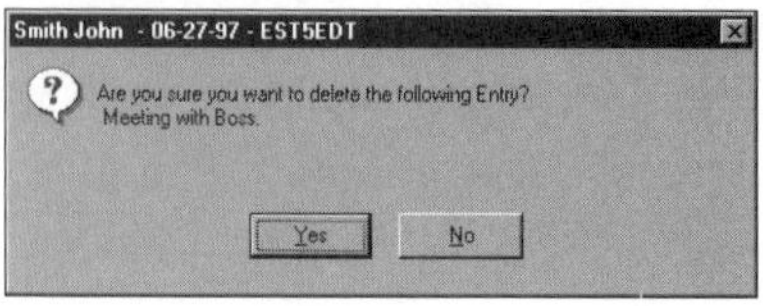

3. Click on Yes.

Your entry is zapped.

Rescheduling an Agenda entry

To reschedule an entry:

1. Double-click on the event. The Edit Entry dialog box appears.

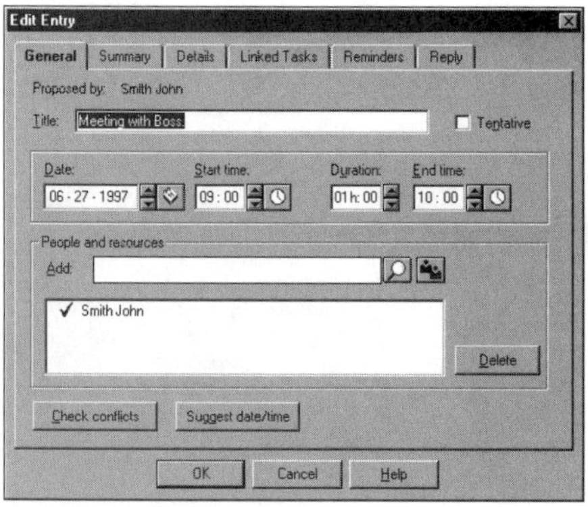

2. Make the necessary changes to the date and time of the event.

3. Click on OK. Calendar notifies all attendees to the event of the revised schedule.

WARNING! You can make changes to only those entries which you have created. Sorry, you can't change the 8:30 a.m. meeting your boss just scheduled for next Monday.

Changing the time slots within the Day view

You can tailor the time slots in Calendar to your needs. For example, if all your appointments are an hour long, then you probably want your Day view in the Agenda to show an hourly breakup of the day. If your appointments vary between half an hour and an hour or more, you may want to have your Day view display the time slots in half-hour increments.

The following two figures show the Day view in one hour time slots and half hour time slots.

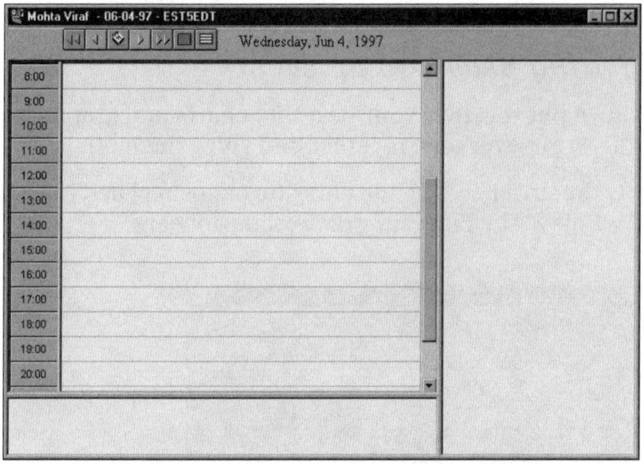

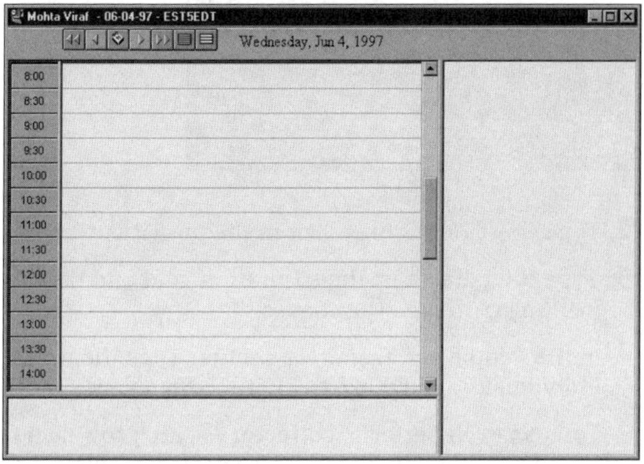

To increase the time allotted to each time slot, click on the Increase Time Slot button in the toolbar (it looks like an alarm clock with a + next to it). The maximum time allocated to a slot is one hour. Remember, this doesn't increase the time allotted to an appointment. It just displays the appointment in a different format.

To decrease the time allotted to each time slot, click on the Decrease Time Slot button in the toolbar (it looks like an alarm clock with a - next to it). The minimum time allocated to a slot is five minutes. Again, this doesn't decrease the time alloted to an apointment. It just displays the time allotted to the appoinment in a different format.

Inviting people to an event

You've put together your beautiful charts and graphs, and now it's time to get everyone together and show them off:

1. Create a new Agenda entry by choosing File⇨New⇨Agenda Entry. The Edit Entry dialog box appears.

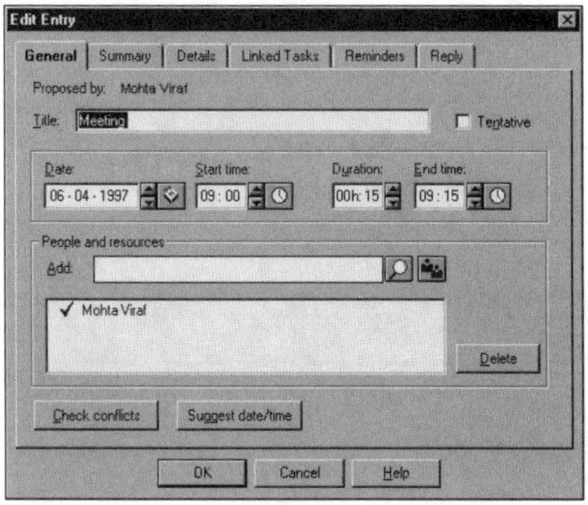

2. Type the Title for the event in the the Title: box.
3. Type the Date, Start time, Duration, and End time for the meeting in the relevant boxes.
4. In the People and resources section, type the name(s) of the individual(s) you'd like to invite to the event.

TIP

You can even perform a directory search to select the person from the company directory. To perform a directory search for an individual's name, click on the search button, the one with the magnifying glass on it. The Directory search dialog box appears.

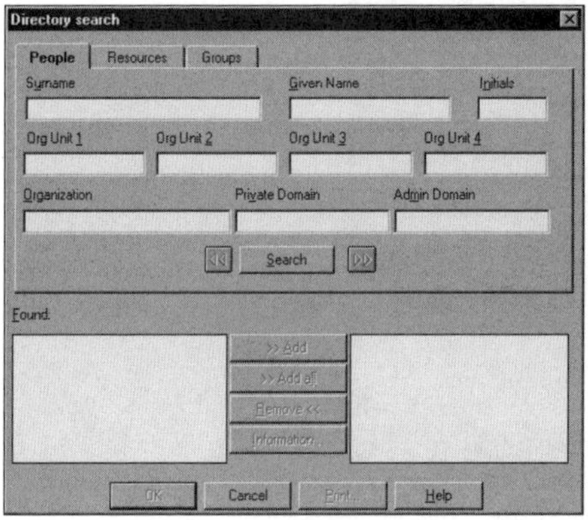

5. Enter the last name of the person you're looking for and click on Search. Select the individual from the Found box and click on Add. This displays the individual's name in the Selected box. Repeat this for all people you want to invite to your meeting. Click on OK. This returns you to the Edit Entry dialog box.

6. Click on Check conflicts to check for scheduling conflicts among the individuals you've invited. If there are any, you will see an X next to the description of the meeting in the box at the bottom of the window.

7. Double-click on the meeting description to get details on the conflicts. The Details of Conflict window appears.

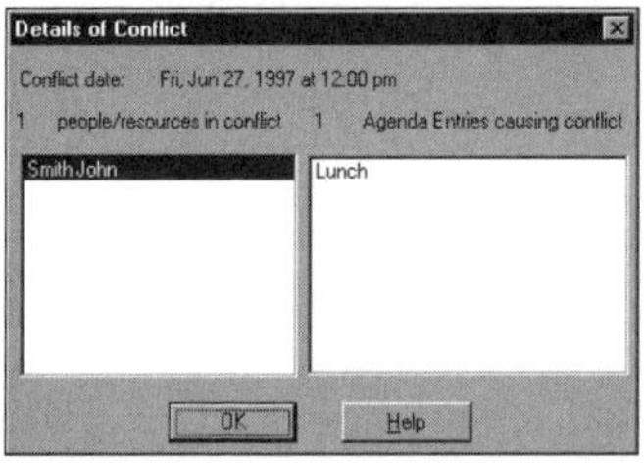

8. Click on OK. This returns you to the Edit Entry dialog box.

9. Click on Suggest date/time to get a suggestion for resolving scheduling conflicts. You see the Suggest Date/Time dialog box.

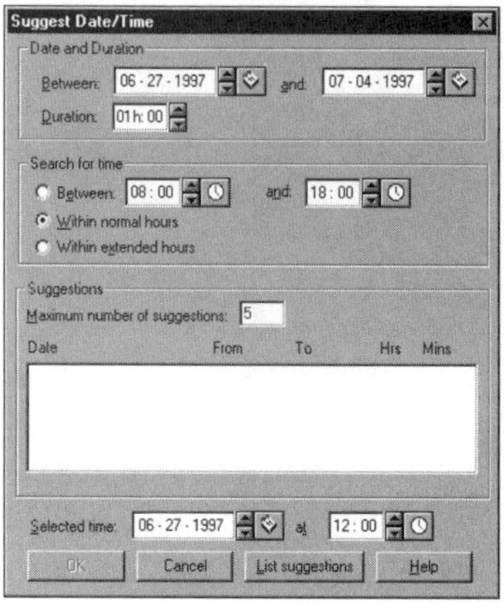

10. In the Date and Duration section, select the appropriate time and duration of your scheduled event.

11. In the Search for time section, select the hours within which you want to find available time.

12. Type the Maximum number of suggestions in the Suggestions section.

13. Click on List Suggestions. A list of available time slots appears in the box within the Suggestions section.

14. Double-click on a suggestion which suits your schedule. This returns you to the Edit Entry window and inserts the suggestion you picked in the appropriate Date, Start time, Duration, and End time boxes.

15. Click on Create. This adds the event to your calendar and also sends notification to all attendees about the meeting. The notification is either an e-mail message or an entry in the recipient In-Tray. ***(See also*** "Setting Notification Options for New Entries.")

Notes

In addition to appointments and schedules, you can add little, or not so little, notes to yourself in Calendar. You may do this to remind yourself of things which you don't care to list as appointments.

Adding a note to the Agenda

To add a note to the Agenda:

1. Click on the Calendar button on the Date Control bar to make the calendar appear.
2. Click on the date for which you want to add a note.
3. Click on the New Daily Note button on the toolbar. The New Daily Note dialog box appears.

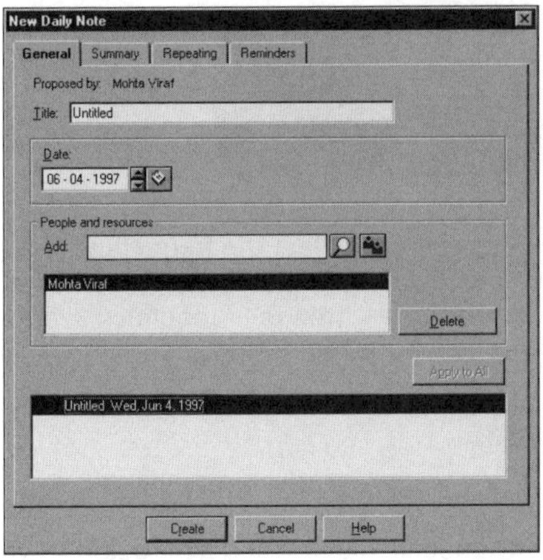

4. Type a Title for the note in the Title box.
5. In the People and resources section, add the people you want the note to be distributed to. To search for specific users or groups to add to the distribution list, click on the Search or Group buttons.
6. If you want the note to be confidential, click on the Summary tab and change the Access option to Confidential.
7. You can have the note displayed on multiple days, such as Mondays and Thursdays of every week, or any such choice. Click on the Repeating tab.

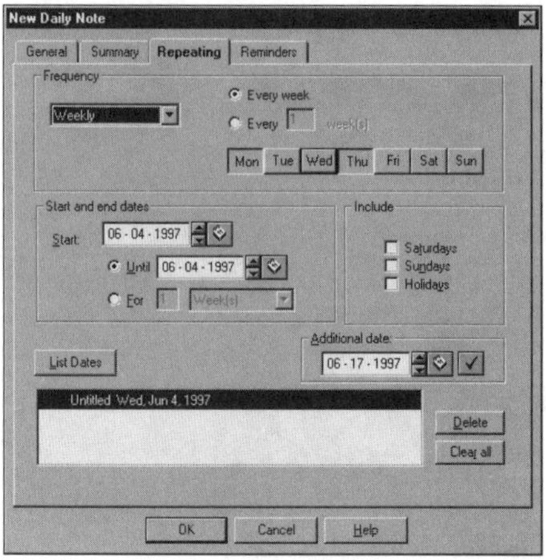

In the Frequency section, select the frequency — day, week, month, year — with which you'd like to repeat the note. Notice how the options within the Frequency section change as you change the Frequency option.

Choose the days of the month or week on which you'd like the note repeated.

Select the start and end dates for the repeating period.

If there are any specific dates you'd like to add to your selection, do so by choosing them in the Additional date box.

Click on List Dates to see all the dates on which the note will be repeated.

8. Click on OK. You see a dialog box asking you if you want to create a list of dates using the current settings.
9. Click on Yes.
10. Click on OK.
11. Click on Create.

The note should now appear in your Day view with a little yellow icon of a note next to it. If you asked it to be repeated on multiple days, the note appears on the Day view of those days, too.

You can create more than one note for any day. Multiple notes for a day appear one below the other in the Notes window.

Creating a duplicate note

You can duplicate or repeat a note which you may have created to have it show up on another day as well.

When you create a note initially, you can repeat it over several days. But after you finish creating a note, you can go back to it and repeat it for only a single day at a time. So if you want to repeat it over ten days, you have to repeat the following procedure ten times. Bummer!

1. Select the note by clicking on it.
2. Choose Edit⇨Duplicate Entry. The Duplicate Entry dialog box appears.

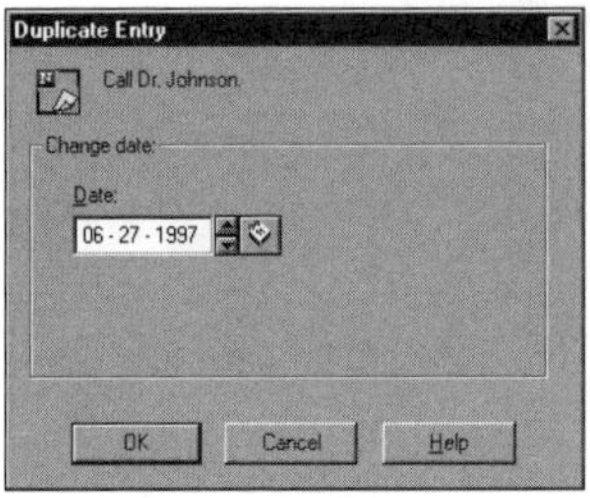

3. Choose a date to which you want to copy the note.
4. Click on OK.

The note is copied to the chosen date.

Printing

Printing your Agenda or your tasks from the Calendar enables you to have a hard copy of your schedule. You can print your Agenda or tasks in a variety of popular formats.

Printing your Agenda

To print your Agenda:

1. Make sure that the view — Day, Week, or Month — you have set your Agenda to is the format in which you want to print. For example, if you want to print a copy of an entire month's Agenda, make sure that the Agenda is in the Month view mode.

- To change to Day view, choose File⇨Day.
- To change to Week view, choose File⇨Week.
- To change to Month view, choose File⇨Month.

2. Using the Date Control toolbar, select the day, week, or month for which you want to print the Agenda.
3. Choose File⇨Print. The Print Dialog box appears.

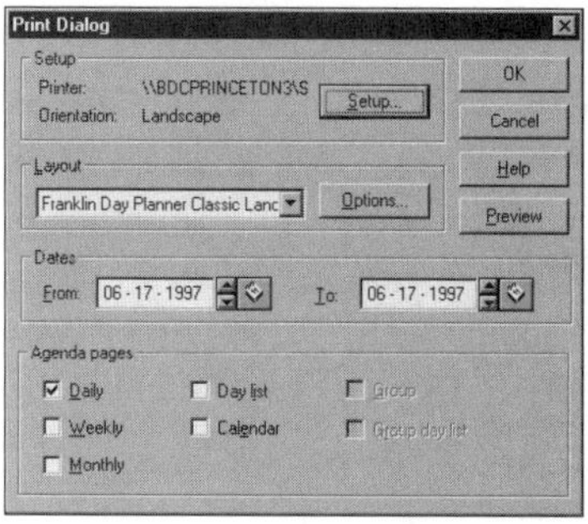

4. Click on the currently selected choice in the Layout section. This displays a drop-down menu, listing several formats in which to print your Agenda.
5. Click on a format to choose it.
6. Click on Options in the layout selection. The Layout Options dialog box appears.

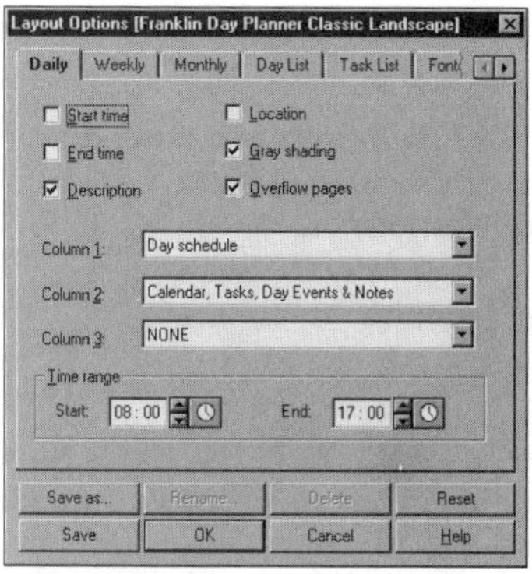

The title bar of the window shows the print format which you've selected.

7. Click on the tab which corresponds to the view option you've selected. Doing so displays various options you can set for that particular view.

8. Select the options you want.

9. Click on OK. You return to the Print Dialog box.

10. Click on Preview to see what your printout will look like.

11. Click on Close to close the Preview window and return to the Print Dialog box.

12. Click on OK.

Copies of your Agenda should be on their way to your printer.

Printing your tasks

To print a task:

1. Click on the Open Tasks button on the Calendar toolbar. The Tasks for window appears with all your tasks listed in it.

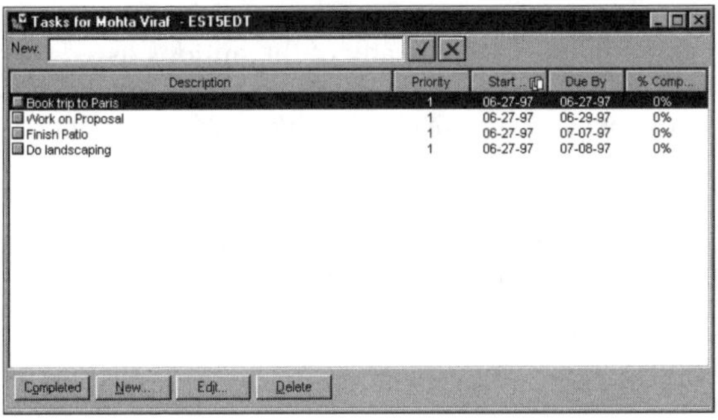

2. You can either print just one task from the list or all the tasks in the list. To print just one task, click on the task you want to print and choose File⇨Print Selected Task. To print all tasks, choose File⇨Print.

   The Print Dialog box appears.

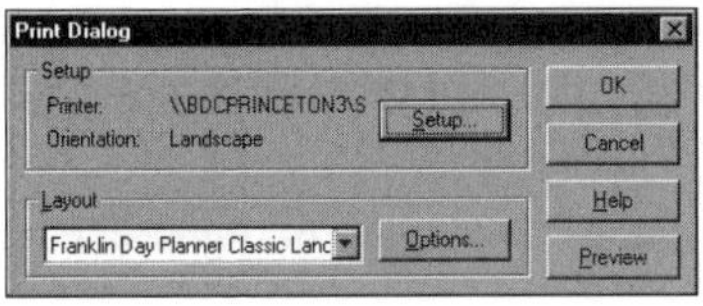

3. Calendar provides you with several print formats, like the Franklin Planner and Day-Timer formats, to print your tasks in. Click on the chosen format in the Layout section. A drop-down menu appears listing the available formats. Select a format.

4. Click on Options in the Layout section. The Layout Options dialog box appears.

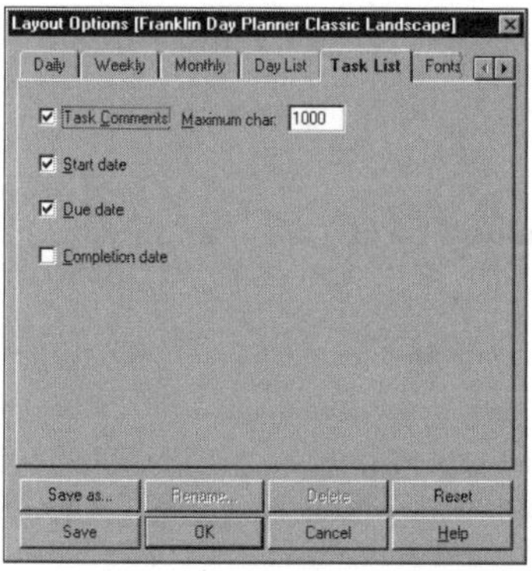

5. If you don't wish to see any of the options listed there in the printed copy of the task list, remove the checkmarks from the checkboxes for those options by clicking on them.

6. Click on OK.

7. Click on Preview to see what the printed copy will look like. The Preview window appears.

8. Click on Close to return to the Print Dialog box.

9. Click on OK.

You should see your task list appear on your printer within seconds.

Setting Notification Options for New Entries

Calendar offers you two options by which you can be notified when someone schedules an event with you as an attendee. You can ask Calendar to send you notification via an e-mail, or you can ask Calendar to send the notification directly to your In-Tray. Here's how you select your notification option:

1. Choose Edit⇨Preferences⇨Agenda. The Agenda Preferences dialog box appears.

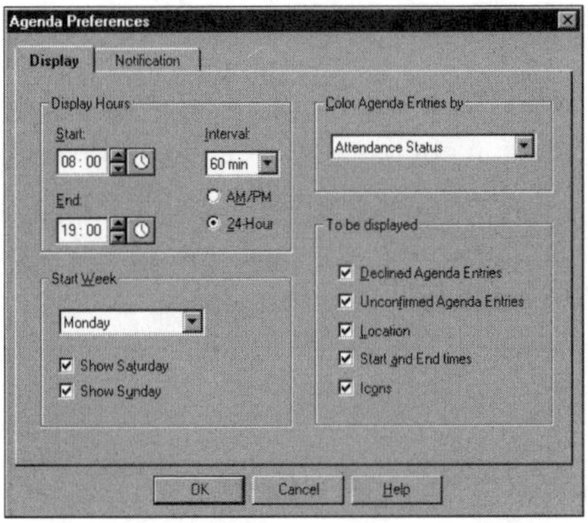

2. Click on the Notification tab.

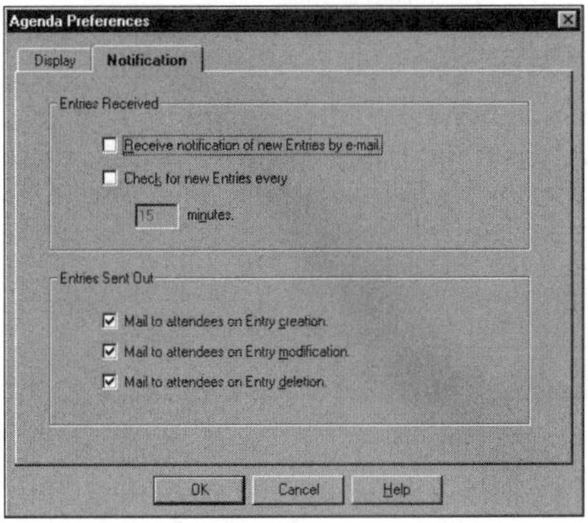

3. In the Entries Received section, select a notification option by clicking on its checkbox.

   If you select the Check for new Entries every option, type the number of minutes in the minutes box indicating how often Calendar should check your Agenda for new event entries. The minimum time interval you can select is 15 minutes.

   If you select the Check for new Entries every option, all new entries appear in your In-Tray. When a new entry is added to your In-Tray, the New Entry icon appears on your Status Bar.

4. Click on OK.

Setting Reminders

Calendar has a sort of alarm clock which reminds you of an upcoming event. You can choose how you like to be reminded:

- ✦ With a pop-up window which is displayed automatically before the event, regardless of what application is currently being used on the computer.
- ✦ With a message which shows up as a note on your Agenda page.

Setting a reminder for an event

To set a reminder for an event:

1. Double-click on the event. The Edit Entry dialog box appears.
2. Click on the Reminders Tab.
3. Click on the Reminder ON: radio button.
4. You can set the Reminder to display a pop-up box reminding you of the event, or have the Reminder display a note in your Agenda. To display a pop-up window, select Pop-Up. To display a note, select Display Upcoming.
5. Click on OK.

Hitting the snooze button to postpone a reminder

Just like the trusted snooze button on your alarm clock, Calendar has a snooze button, too. When a pop-up reminder window pops up to remind you of an event, you can ask it to remind you again in the next few minutes or hours:

1. Click on Snooze within the Reminder pop-up window.

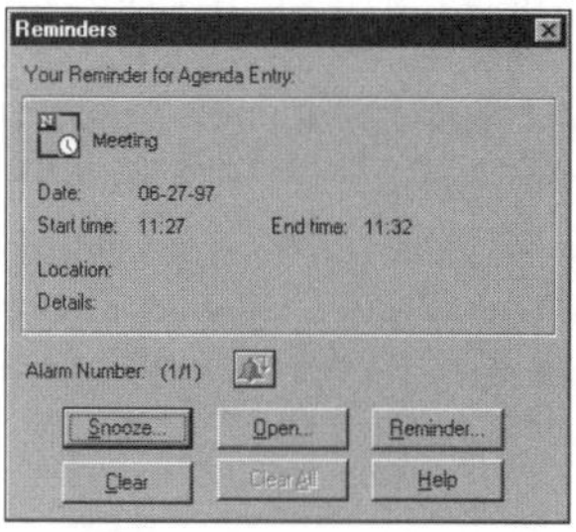

The Snooze Alert window appears.

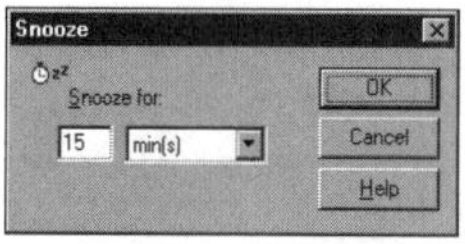

2. Specify the number of minutes or hours after which you want the Reminder to remind you again.
3. Click on OK.

Turning reminders off and on

You can temporarily turn off all reminders for a specfic period of time and then turn them on again later. You may want to do this if you're going to use your computer to make an overhead presentation to a group of people, and you don't want the reminders to pop up in the midst of your presentation.

To turn off your reminders, choose View⇨Turn Reminders Off.

To turn on your reminders, choose View⇨Turn Reminders On.

Toolbars

Calendar offers two toolbars. One is the Calendar toolbar, and the other is the Date Control bar.

Calendar toolbar

You find the Calendar toolbar right under the menu bar in the Netscape Calendar window. The toolbar provides one-click access to the tools used within the Agenda. You can choose to either hide the toolbar or to display it. To hide it, choose View⇨Toolbar. To turn it on again, choose View⇨Toolbar again.

The following table tells you what each of the buttons in the toolbar does.

Toolbar Button	What It Does
	Opens your In-Tray
	Opens an Agenda
	Displays your tasks
	Opens the Agenda pages for several users

(continued)

Toolbar Button	What It Does
	Finds an In-Tray entry in your Daily Agenda pages
	Displays the Daily Agenda page
	Displays the Weekly Agenda page
	Displays the Monthly Agenda page
	Decreases the time slot in your Agenda pages
	Increases the time slot in your Agenda pages
	Lets you turn on or turn off certain icons in the Agenda pages and Task display
	Changes the colors of your Agenda entries
	Opens a New Agenda Entry
	Creates a new task
	Creates a new day event
	Creates a new daily note
	Prints Agenda pages, task lists, and other Calendar entries

Date Control bar

You find the Date Control bar across the top of your Agenda page window.

Depending on which Agenda view you are in — Day view, Week view, Month view — the toolbar's buttons perform different functions. The following table lists each button in the toolbar along with its function.

Toolbar Button	What It Does
	Moves you back one week in the Day view, one month in the Week view, and six months in the Month view within your Agenda pages
	Moves you back one day in the Day view, one week in the Week view, and one month in the Month view within your Agenda pages

Toolbar Button	*What It Does*
	Displays a calendar from which you can pick a date to go to in the Agenda
	Moves you forward one day in the Day view, one week in the Week view, and one month in the Month view within your Agenda pages
	Moves you forward one week in the Day view, one month in the Week view, and six months in the Month view within your Agenda pages
	Displays more entries within the Day view Agenda by decreasing the height of the rows within it
	Displays fewer entries within the Day view Agenda by increasing the height of the rows within it

Tracking Tasks

In addition to an Agenda entry such as a meeting or an appointment, you can add tasks to your Agenda. A task could be something like a project you have to work on, or a letter you have to write, or something similar which you wouldn't usually schedule as an appointment in your Agenda.

Adding a task

To add a task to your Agenda:

1. Use the Calendar button on the Date Control bar to go to the day in which you want to add the task. The Agenda appears showing the selected day.
2. Double-click in the Task Display window. The New Task dialog box appears.

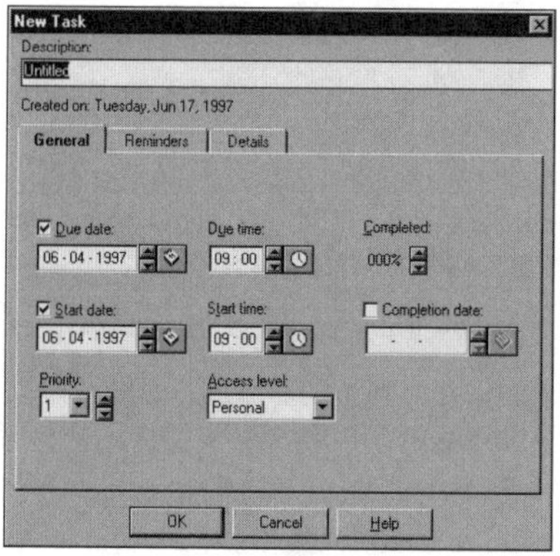

3. Type a description of the task in the Description box.

   You do not need to specify a due date, start date, or even completion date if any of them are not necessary. Specify them if they are critical to the task.

4. Click on the Reminders tab if you'd like to set reminders for the task and specify the times you'd like to be reminded.
5. Click on the Details tab. A Comments box appears within the Details tab.
6. Type a description for the Task. You may leave this blank if you choose to.
7. Click on OK.

The task should now appear in the Task window.

Editing a task

To edit a task:

1. Double-click on the task. The Edit Task dialog box appears.

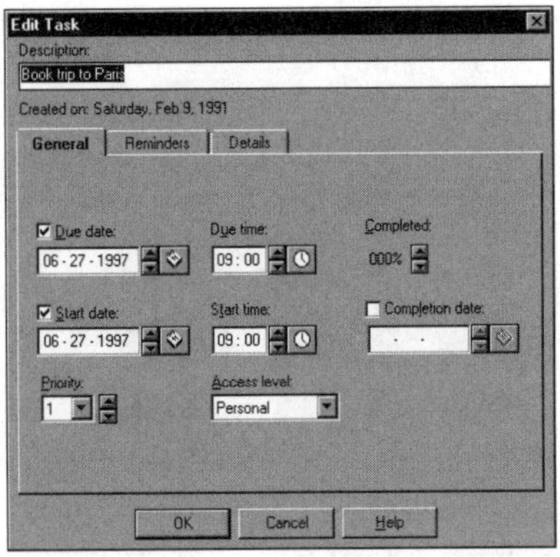

2. Make the necessary changes to the task.
3. Click on OK.

Assigning a status to a task

The box next to a task in the Task window indicates the status of the task:

✦ A square with a check mark in it indicates that the task has been completed.

- A square with no check mark in it means that work on the task hasn't begun yet.
- A percentage number in parentheses next to the square indicates that you have completed that percentage of the task.
- A red border around a square indicates that the task is overdue.

To change the status of a task:

1. Double-click on the task in the Task window. The Edit Task dialog box appears.
2. Using the up and down arrows under Completed: to indicate what percentage of the task has been completed.
3. Click on OK. Notice the change in the task status indicator in the Task window for the modified task.

Viewing all your tasks

You can view all the tasks in your Agenda, which may be spread over the entire calendar, in a single window. You can see the status of all tasks at a glance, edit them, and create new tasks, all from within a single window:

1. Choose File⇨Open Tasks⇨Your Tasks. All your tasks appear in a separate window.

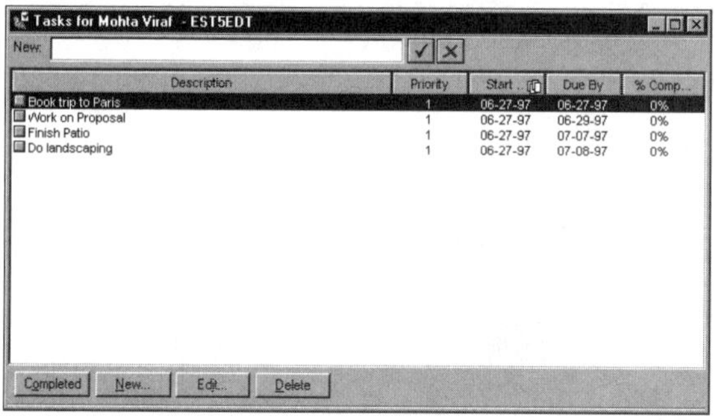

2. To edit a task, double-click on it. The Edit Task dialog box appears.
3. Make the necessary changes and click on OK.
4. Choose File⇨Close to close the window.

Viewing other people's tasks

You can view other people's tasks if you have been granted the access privileges to do so, but you can't edit them. To view someone else's task:

1. Choose File⇨Open Tasks⇨View Other's Tasks. The User Selection dialog box appears, asking for the name of the user whose tasks you want to view.

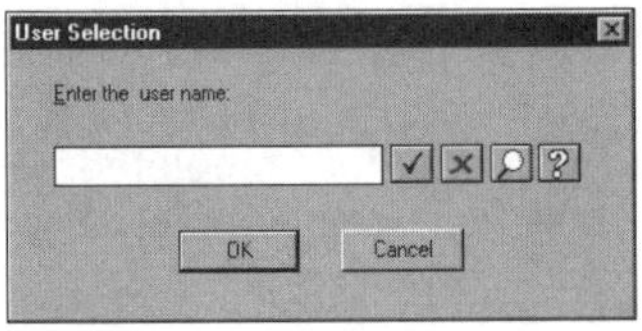

2. Enter the name of the user.
3. Click on OK. The specified user's Task window appears.
4. When you finish viewing the user's Tasks, choose File⇨Close to close the window.

Viewing Another User's Agenda

You can view another user's Agenda as long as you have been granted the access rights to do so. Assuming you have the access rights, here's how you'd view the person's Agenda:

1. Choose File⇨Open Agenda⇨And Agenda. The Open an Agenda dialog box appears.

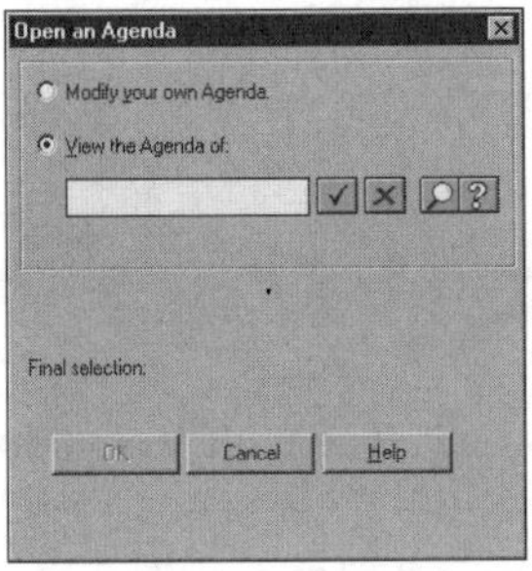

2. Make sure the radio button next to View the Agenda of is selected. Type the name of the user in the box provided. If you don't know the exact name of the individual, you can perform

a directory search using the Search button, which has a magnifying glass on it.

3. Press Enter.

The chosen user's Agenda appears.

Viewing Your Calendar

A view within Calendar is the format in which your Agenda is displayed. You could choose to display the Agenda in one of three views — Day, Week, or Month.

Day view

To display your Agenda in Day view format, choose File➪Day. The Agenda appears in glorious Day view.

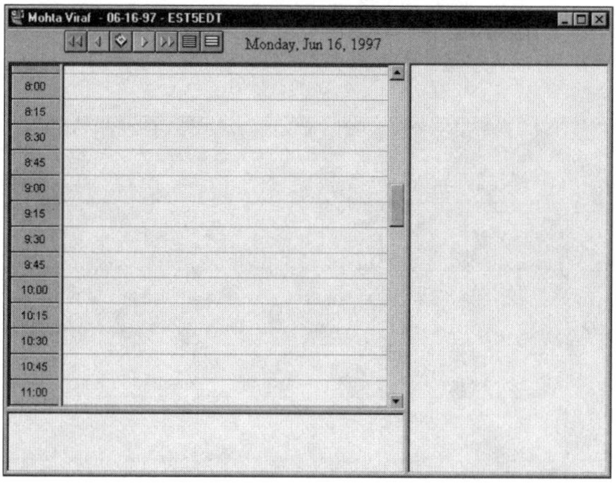

Week view

To display your Agenda in Week view format, choose, File➪Week. The Agenda appears in Week view.

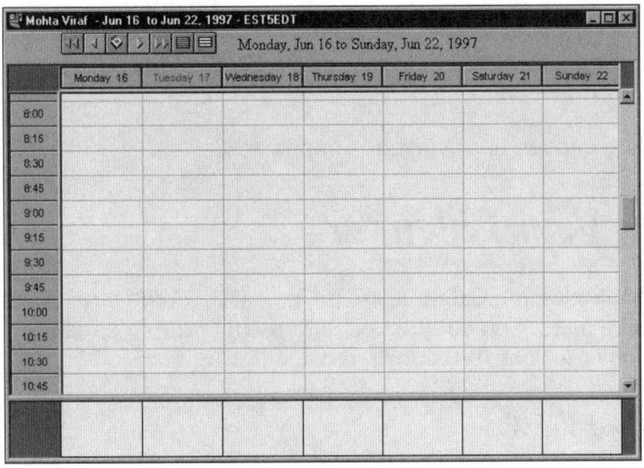

Month view

To display your Agenda in Month view format, choose File⇨Month. Guess what view the Agenda appears in?

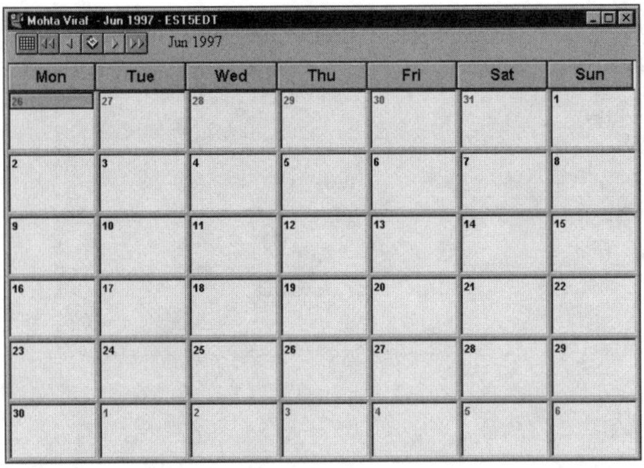

Working with the In-Tray

The In-Tray shows you all entries which you have received from or sent to other users. These include entries you have accepted, sent out, or refused or haven't responded to yet.

Follow these steps to view just the entries you want to see:

1. Choose File⇨Open In-Tray. The In-Tray appears.

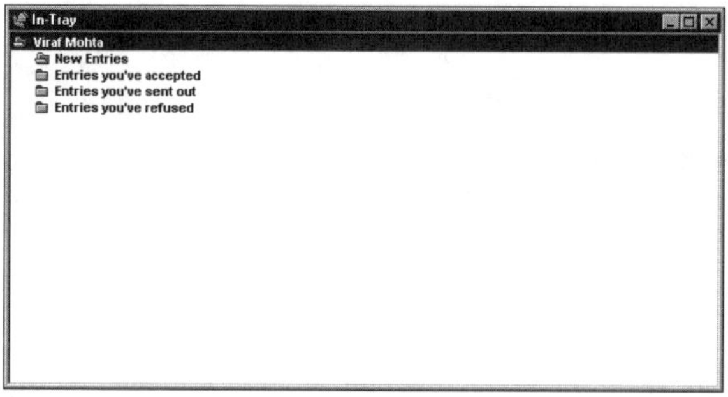

The following folders appear in the In-Tray:

- **New Entries:** These are entries which have newly arrived in the In-Tray.
- **Entries you've accepted:** These are entries which had arrived earlier and which you accepted.
- **Entries you've sent out:** These are entries you sent out to other individuals.
- **Entries you've refused:** These are entries which you received but refused.

2. Click on the folder that contains the type of entry you wish to see.
3. The folder opens, listing all entries within it.
4. To close the folder, click on it again.
5. To close the In-Tray, choose File⇨Close.

Part VIII

IBM Host On-Demand

Those among us who haven't been using computers for long may be unaware that the world of computers is made up of little computers like the ones we have on our desks, and big computers, called *mainframes,* which are way too big to put on our desks. For most, if not all, of the work we do, the ones on our desks do just fine. But there are times when some of us have to use the big ones hidden behind the locked doors of the "computer room." And we do so using a special computer terminal, called a 3270 terminal, which is used for connecting to IBM mainframes only. Or we use special software, called *terminal emulators,* installed on our desktop computers which make our desktops resemble the terminals.

Communicator comes equipped with special software to let you connect with IBM mainframes right from within your browser. This component of Communicator is IBM Host On-Demand, which is only available in the Professional version of Communicator.

In this part . . .

- **Starting an IBM Host On-Demand session**
- **Starting a second host session**
- **Getting acquainted with the IBM Host On-Demand keyboard**

Starting an IBM Host On-Demand Session

To start an IBM Host On-Demand session and connect to an IBM mainframe computer:

1. Choose Communicator⇨IBM Host On-Demand. The Host On-Demand window appears.

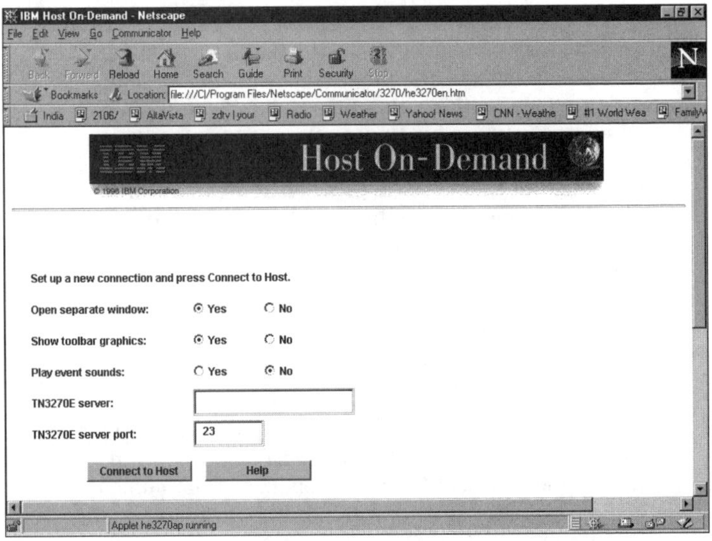

2. You may leave the first three option settings with their default values. But if you absolutely have to tinker with them, here's an explanation of what each one means:

   - **Open separate window:** Shows the mainframe screen in a new window, allowing you to resize the window if you need to make it larger or smaller. If you don't open a separate window, the host session appears in the browser window. In this case, you can't resize the session window, but you can scroll the browser window if necessary.
   - **Show toolbar graphics:** Shows the toolbar buttons in the mainframe window with graphics.
   - **Play event sounds:** Plays sounds when an event takes place within the mainframe window.

3. Enter the TN3270E server address and the TN3270E server port in the relevant boxes. You can obtain this information from your network administrator.

4. Click on Connect to host. You see the Host window. After a successful connection has been made, Host On-Demand presents you with login information for your specific host.

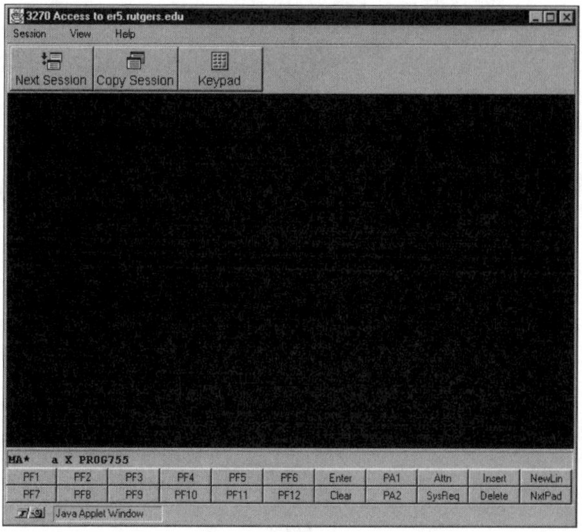

5. Log in to the host and continue your host session.

6. To end the session, choose Session⇨Exit.

Starting Your Second Host Session

You can have a maximum of two host sessions running at the same time from within IBM Host On-Demand.

To start a second host session:

1. Go to the screen of the current session.

2. Click on Copy Session. This starts the second session in a new window.

3. To switch from one session to another, click on Next Session on the toolbar.

4. To end the session, choose Session⇨Exit.

Working with the IBM Host On-Demand Keyboard

The IBM 3270 terminal keyboard has a whole bunch of keys which are normally unavailable on the regular personal computer keyboard. To use these keys, you can use the keyboard toolbar at the bottom of the host screen when you are logged on to a host session. The following table lists the key combinations for using your keyboard's keys to emulate the 3270 keyboard.

3270 Function Keys	*Keyboard Keys*
F1-F12	F1-F12
F13-F24	Shift+F1-Shift+12
Cursor Left	Left arrow
Cursor Right	Right arrow
Cursor Up	Up arrow
Cursor Down	Down arrow
Delete	Delete
Backspace	Backspace
Forward Tab	Tab
Back Tab	Shift+Tab
Enter	Enter
Clear	Esc
PA1	Home
End	End
Character keys	Character keys

Techie Talk

address: A unique identifier for an individual or a Web site on the Internet.

Address Book: A file on your computer which contains e-mail addresses.

AIFF (Audio Interchange File Format): A format, developed by Apple Computer, for storing audio clips.

algorithm: A sequence of actions, usually mathematical, performed to obtain a desired result. When a plain text message is encrypted, an algorithm converts the text to secret code. When the text is decrypted, another algorithm performs the necessary task to convert the secret code to plain text.

anonymous remailer: A Web site that automatically forwards your message to another person or newsgroup, stripping your e-mail address, and therefore your identity, from the message. Great for sending love letters to your boss.

ASCII (American Standard Code for Information Interchange): Pronounced *as-key.* A set of characters which includes the letters, numbers, and special characters on a regular English keyboard. An ASCII file (also called a plain text file) refers to a file made up of just these characters, a file which can be read by any software program.

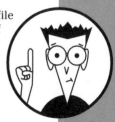

at sign (@): A standard component of any e-mail address that separates the mailbox name from the domain name.

attach: Send a file along with an e-mail message, which allows you to maintain any special formatting contained in the file.

attachment: The file attached to an e-mail message. An attachment can be a text file, picture file, or even a sound file.

AutoAdmin: A feature in Netscape Communicator that automatically checks to see that your computer is using the most current version of certain programs. The feature automatically supplies the most recent version of the programs to your machine if it is not already running them.

Bcc (Blind Carbon Copy): An address option which allows you to send a copy of a message to someone without his or her name or address appearing on the message form.

beta product: A product which is undergoing testing and is not yet ready for the market. A software product could go through several beta versions before it's finally released.

BIOS (Basic Input Output System): A part of the computer's operating system which provides an interface between a computer and the devices it is connected to, such as the monitor, keyboard, and mouse.

bit: The smallest unit of computer data.

bitmap (BMP): An image format in which the height and width of an image is characterized by a number of pixels. An image stored in this format has the BMP extension.

bookmark: A marker placed in your browser for a Web site you just visited and may want to visit in the future. Keeping bookmarks of sites saves you from typing in the address for the site each time you want to visit it. Bookmarking proves a great research tool because you can categorize your bookmarked sites by topic.

bounce: To redirect an e-mail message to another recipient.

bps (bits per second): A measure of the speed with which information is transmitted from one computer to another.

browser: A computer program with which you can view documents and images on the Web. Netscape Navigator is an example of a browser.

bug: A computer error. The origin of the term is traced to a computer malfunction which was caused by an insect being trapped in the computer's electrical circuit.

bus: The pathway within a computer on which data flows. The width of a bus determines the size, in bits, of the largest piece of data it can carry. A 16-bit bus can carry data in 16-bit chunks, whereas a 32-bit bus can carry data in 32-bit chunks.

byte: A collection of bits, usually 8, which make up a character.

cache: An area in the computer's memory which stores frequently accessed information.

Calendar: Component of Netscape Communicator which lets you schedule meetings, appointments, and events. ***See*** Part VII.

call waiting: A telephone service that you must disable while your phone line is connected to your modem.

case-sensitive: Usually applied to search functions, a feature that distinguishes terms by their capitalization. For example, a search function that is case sensitive distinguishes between the words *Business* and *business*.

Cc (Carbon Copy): An address option that allows you to send a message to more than one person at once.

channel: On IRC, a place where a group of people gather to discuss a specific topic, such as parenting on ParentChat. Within Netcaster, a source of news, such as ABC News.

chat: Ability to conduct a live text-based discussion with another Web user. ***See*** Part VI.

collaborative browsing: Process by which you and another Web user browse the Web together, simultaneously going to the same Web sites. ***See*** Part VI.

Collabra: Component of Netscape Communicator which lets you participate in newsgroups or discussion groups. ***See*** Part IV.

Communicator: Groupware software from Netscape Corporation which includes Navigator, Messenger, Collabra, Composer, Conference, Calendar, and IBM Host On-Demand. ***See*** Part I.

component: Another word for program, often used to refer to the various programs that comprise a groupware package. For example, Netscape Calendar is a component of Netscape Communicator.

Component bar: Toolbar within Communicator which allows easy access to various components within Communicator.

Composer: Component of Netscape Communicator which lets you create Web pages. ***See*** Part V.

compressed file: A file which has been made smaller without deleting anything within it, so that it occupies less space on a floppy disk or hard-drive. Also, a file which contains several files within it.

compression utility: Software, such as WinZip, with which you can compress a file or package several files into one file.

Conference: Component of Netscape Communicator which lets you and another person browse the Web together, use a white-board to view and edit graphics, conduct live phone and text conversations, and exchange electronic files easily. ***See*** Part VI.

cookie: A tiny packet of information, sent by a Web server to your browser when you visit the server for the first time. The browser then sends back the cookie to the server each time you access that server. Cookies identify you to the server.

CPU (Central Processing Unit): The main part or chip within a computer which controls all the operations of the computer.

cracker: An individual who accesses a computer system without proper authorization, with malicious intent. Often erroneously called a *hacker.*

cross-posting: Simultaneously posting a news article to more than one newsgroup. Don't cross-post unless you're sure that your information is pertinent to all the newsgroups.

Cyberspace: The millions of computers all around the world that are connected together to form the abstract world of the Internet.

decryption: The process by which encrypted information is converted back to normal text.

default: A setting or option that Netscape Communicator automatically sets, thinking that most people will need or will choose that setting or option in order to do their work. Most default options in Netscape Communicator can be changed.

dialog box: Feature of most software programs that allows you to choose or specify certain options in a window.

DNS (Domain Name Server): A system on the Internet which converts a Web site's address from its easy-to-remember address, like `www.dummies.com`, to its numerical form. DNS saves you the trouble of remembering the lengthy numerical form of the address.

domain: A category to which a Web site belongs. A Web site's domain is identifiable by the last three digits of the site's URL or Web address. Examples of domains are `mil` (for military sites), `edu` (for educational sites), `com` (for commercial sites), `org` (for non-profit sites), and `gov` (for government sites).

domain name: A name which uniquely identifies a computer on the Internet. No two computers can have the same domain name.

download: Copy a program or file from another computer to your computer.

draft: A feature in Netscape Messenger that allows you to begin an e-mail message and then save the message for completion at a later time.

drag-and-drop: A feature in Netscape Communicator that lets you perform a certain task by highlighting an icon on the screen and then dragging it, using your mouse, to another location on the screen. For example, if you want to print a document, you can drag the icon representing the document and then drop it over the printer icon on the screen.

easter egg: An undocumented command in a computer program intended as a joke. For example, an easter egg in the Windows 3.1 program displays the names of all the programmers who worked on the program.

e-mail: Message sent by an individual to another over a computer network.

e-mail address: An electronic address for an individual or entity on the Internet or a LAN, to which e-mail can be sent.

emoticons: Little pictures that you can include in your e-mails to express emotions and special messages. For example, the following emoticon expresses humor: <g>.

encryption: Process by which a text file can be coded and made unreadable to prevent unauthorized people from reading it. To make an encrypted message readable again, you need to know the password with which it was encrypted.

FAQ (Frequently Asked Question): A set of frequently asked questions with answers relating to a specific program, Web site, or newsgroup.

filtering: A feature in Netscape Messenger that allows you to automatically send messages from a particular source to a specified location (usually a folder) on your computer.

finger: A program which lets you find information about another individual on the Internet.

firewall: A program which acts as a gate between an organization's internal computer network and the Internet, preventing Internet users from accessing the organization's computer network but letting the organization's employees access the Internet.

flame: An impolite, insulting, and inflammatory e-mail message or post on a newsgroup. Avoid flames by adhering to the rules of Internet etiquette.

freeware: Software that is totally free for you to use. You can download tons of freeware from the Internet.

FTP (File Transfer Protocol): A set of guidelines governing the transfer of files from one computer to another on the Internet.

GIF (Graphics Interchange Format): A graphics format, introduced by CompuServe. GIF images have the GIF extension.

groupware: Computer software which contains components for a variety of functions, such as scheduling, e-mail, and conferencing.

hacker: An individual obsessed with computer technology. One who finds joy in unearthing the nitty-gritty behind the workings of computers, without malicious intent. Often erroneously called a *cracker.*

highlight: An action you must perform (usually by clicking) on an item before selecting an option that modifies the item.

History file: A record of the Web sites you have visited in the recent past.

home page: A location on the World Wide Web which has a specific URL.

host: Usually a large computer on a network to which other smaller computers are connected.

hostname: The URL or Web address of a site in its easy-to-remember form, such as `www.dummies.com`, rather than in its numerical equivalent.

HTML (HyperText Markup Language): The language used to create Web pages. HTML uses tags such as <Bold> and <Center> to specify how text should be displayed. It also has tags to specify hypertext links and include images within a document.

HTTP (HyperText Transfer Protocol): An Internet protocol with which a Web server receives requests for documents and sends the documents over to the requester.

hypertext: Text which contains linked words, called *hyperlinks,* which let you jump to another section or document containing related information.

IBM Host On-Demand: Component of Navigator through which you can connect to an IBM mainframe computer. ***See*** Part VIII.

interface: An abstract layer or boundary between a computer and a human, between computer systems, or within various parts of a software program.

Internet: A network of computer networks which spans the globe, allowing people from all parts of the world to communicate with each other.

Internet address: The numerical address of a Web site on the Internet.

InterNIC (Internet Network Information Center): Organization which is responsible for assigning Internet domain names in the U.S. Its Web site is at `www.internic.com`.

intranet: A network within an organization, available only to its employees, and one which uses the same communication protocols as the Internet. You can use Communicator almost identically regardless of whether you are on the Internet or on your company's intranet.

In-Tray: In Netscape Calendar, a feature that shows you all entries which you have received from or sent to other users. These include entries you have accepted, sent out, refused, or haven't responded to yet.

IP (Internet Protocol): A standard of communication for computers on the Internet.

IRC (Internet Relay Chat): A feature of the Internet which lets one or more Internet users participate in a live text-based discussion.

ISDN (Integrated Services Digital Network): A telephone service over which voice and data can be simultaneously carried.

ISP (Internet Service Provider): A company which, for a fee, provides Internet services, including e-mail and access to the World Wide Web. America Online and AT&T WorldNet Service are examples of ISPs.

Java: A programming language developed by Sun Microsystems which is used on the Internet to create programs which are downloaded to a user's computer and executed there. A Java program can be run on any computer system.

JPEG (Joint Photographic Experts Group): Pronounced *Jay-peg.* A group which came up with a format for compressing and storing images. Images that use this format have the JPG extension.

LAN (Local Area Network): A network of computers within a company, over which employees communicate with each other.

launch: Usually used in connection with programs, a computer nerd term that means to open or run the program.

link: A word or image which when clicked on connects to and displays another, related document or image. You navigate the World Wide Web through links.

mailing list: A list containing the e-mail addresses of several individuals. The individuals are known as *subscribers* to the mailing list. When an e-mail message is sent to a specific address, all members of the mailing list automatically receive the message.

marking: In Netscape Collabra, the act of flagging a particular post so that you can find it more easily within the message thread at a later time.

Messenger: Component of Netscape Communicator which lets you send and read and e-mail. ***See*** Part III.

Microsoft Office: A popular groupware package that contains Word, Excel, and PowerPoint, among other programs. Netscape Navigator allows you to view documents created by Microsoft Office programs.

modem (MOdulator-DEModulator): A device which allows a computer to send and receive information from another computer over telephone lines. You hear the modem "singing" when you establish an Internet connection.

multimedia: Information presented in a variety of formats such as audio, video, pictures, and text.

multi-user settings: A feature in Netscape Communicator that allows your coworkers or family members to retain their preferences, such as personalized bookmarks.

MUD (Multi-User Dungeon): A program on the Internet which presents an environment within which you can assume a fictional identity and interact with your surroundings and with other individuals within it.

Navigation toolbar: Toolbar within Navigator which lets you perform several actions within Navigator, such as move back and forth between Web sites and print information.

Navigator: Component of Netscape Communicator which lets you browse the Web. ***See*** Part II.

Net Search: A feature in Netscape Navigator that offers access to several Web-site searching services, intended to help you find what you want on the Web very quickly.

Netcaster: Component of Netscape Communicator with which you receive automatic news updates from various sources on the Internet. ***See*** Part I.

NetHelp: Online help provided by Netscape Communicator from within any of its components.

network: A collection of computers connected to each other, allowing information to flow easily from one computer to another.

newbie: A new user on the Internet. Newbies often distinguish themselves by posing a question on a newsgroup which was just answered the day before.

news reader: A software program with which you can access newsgroups on the Internet.

news server: A computer on the Internet which carries or hosts newsgroups.

newsgroup: An electronic forum on the Internet devoted to the discussion of a specific subject. There are approximately 16,000 newsgroups on the Internet. ***See*** Usenet.

notes: In Netscape Calendar, a feature that allows you to record detailed information about a meeting, task, or event.

packet: A small of amount of data. Data, such as an e-mail message, when sent across the Internet, is not sent as one big chunk. It is broken up into tiny packets which are then put together at the destination.

page: Also called a *home page* or a *Web page.* A location with a unique address on the Internet or an intranet.

password: A secret word or phrase that you may need to type in to gain access to a Web site, network, or computer.

Personal toolbar: Toolbar within Netscape Navigator which has buttons for specific Web sites. These buttons allow you to go to frequently visited Web sites with one click.

pixel: Short for Picture Element. The smallest area of a picture as displayed on a computer screen.

platform: A system standard, such as a PC or a Mac. Netscape Communicator is available for a variety of platforms, including Windows 3.1, Windows 95, Windows NT, Macintosh, PowerPC, and UNIX systems.

plug-in: A software program which when used with a browser allows you to view text, graphics, or video, or listen to audio on the Internet. RealAudio Player is a plug-in which (when used with a browser) lets you listen to music on the Internet created and transmitted in the RealAudio format.

post: A message that appears on a newsgroup. Also, the act of publishing a message to a newsgroup.

PPP (Point-to-Point Protocol): Protocol used for dial-up connections on the Internet. Replaced SLIP as the protocol of choice.

preferences: Options that you can set that customize your Netscape Communicator experience.

property: Fancy-schmancy computer word for the characteristics that make up an item on your computer.

protocol: A set of standards or specifications related to the operation and workings of a computer system or network.

pull: Process by which a user specifically requests information from a Web server by clicking on a link on a page.

push: Process by which a Web server automatically sends information, such as a stock quote, at periodic intervals to a user's browser without the user specifically requesting the information each time.

QuickTime: Format for saving video clips. Developed by Apple Corporation.

raise: What you may get from your boss after you master the efficiency tools available in Netscape Communicator.

RAM (Random Access Memory): The memory used by the computer to store information for fast access. Information is stored in RAM only when the computer is being used, unlike information stored on a floppy disk or hard-drive. Today's software applications require at least 8 MB of RAM, although 16 MB is what you'd need for improved performance.

RealAudio: One of many software programs which lets you listen to audio on the Internet.

reload: The process by which you make a browser request the latest information on a Web page that you are viewing from a Web server.

reminder: In Netscape Calendar, a feature that places either a pop-up window on your computer screen or a message in your Agenda to jog your memory regarding a particular event.

rich text: Text which contains either special fonts, hypertext, or graphics. Text formatted with a word processor is said to be rich text. This is the opposite of plain text, also called ASCII.

ROM (Read Only Memory): A memory device, the contents of which can't be changed once they've been written to the device. An example of such a device is a CD, which you can read from, but can't write to.

rule: A feature in Netscape Communicator that allows you to filter e-mail messages from a particular source into a specified location on your computer (or into your trash).

script: A software program which can be run on the Web within a browser.

search engine: A software program with which you to search for information through a set of documents. Alta Vista is a search engine, and so is Lycos. You specify the word or phrase you're looking for, and the search engine goes through a collection of documents and presents a list of documents containing your search request.

secure server: A server which limits access to certain individuals only, via a name and password check. Most servers are not secure.

security certificate: An electronic ID issued to you by an agency for secure communication on the Internet. The certificate allows you to send and receive encrypted information on the Internet.

SGML (Standard Generalized Markup Language): A language used for creating Web pages and printed documents. HTML is a subset of SGML.

shareware: Software which you can try before you buy. You can try it for free, usually for a month, after which you must pay for it if you decide to continue using it.

S-HTTP (Secure-HTTP): A protocol used by Web sites which transmit sensitive and confidential data on the Internet.

SmartUpdate: A feature in Netscape Communicator that automatically downloads and installs Netcaster, which is a type of news service.

SMTP (Simple Mail Transport Protocol): A standard which lets people send and receive e-mail over the Internet in spite of the vast number of e-mail software packages used around the world.

spell checker: A feature in Netscape Communicator that can save you the embarrassment of misspelling a word in your e-mail or on your Web site. ***See*** Part III.

spider: Also called a *crawler, robot,* or *bot.* A program which roams the Web and automatically downloads documents. A spider can be set to download all links referenced within a document, and then all links referenced within those links, too.

SQL (Structured Query Language): Pronounced *sequel.* Language for accessing databases.

subscribing: In Netscape Collabra, the act of signing up to receive the threaded chat of a specific newsgroup.

surfing: Roaming the Internet.

SysAdmin (System Administrator): Individual in charge of a computer network. This is the person in your company whom you can call when something goes wrong with your computer. Also called a *guru.*

TCP/IP (Transmission Control Protocol/Internet Protocol): Standard which is used to transmit data over the Internet.

telephony: Software which allows you to use your computer for audio communication, like a telephone.

telnet: Computer program which lets you log on to a remote system and use the system as if you were logged in locally. Many library card catalogs can be accessed through telnet, for example.

template: In Netscape Composer, a feature that provides a ready-made Web page that you can customize for your purposes. ***See*** Part V.

thread: A discussion on a newsgroup relating to a specific subject. A thread is comprised of a message plus all the responses to the message.

TIFF (Tagged Image File Format): A file format used for bitmap images. A TIFF file has the TIF extension.

toolbar: A bar available in a window that contains a number of buttons. Clicking a button on a toolbar performs some function within the program.

tracking: A feature in Netscape Messenger that allows you to see which Web sites you have visited.

uncompress: Process by which a compressed file is expanded to its original size or made to release the several files packaged within it.

upload: Copy a program or file from your computer to another computer.

URL (Uniform Resource Locator): A unique address of a computer or file on the Internet. `www.dummies.com` is a URL.

Usenet: A collection of newsgroups on the Internet. There are over 16,000 newsgroups on Usenet covering a wide rage of topics — everything from apples to zoos.

virus: A malicious computer program which destroys data on a computer. Like a common virus which can stay undetected in your body, a computer virus can stay hidden on your computer and can replicate itself. Scary.

voice mail: A message left on a telephone answering machine. In Netscape Communicator, a recorded audio message sent within an e-mail message. ***See*** Part VI.

VRML (Virtual Reality Modeling Language): An extension of HTML with which one can simulate a 3-D effect on the Web.

Wav: Pronounced *wave.* A format for saving audio clips developed by Microsoft.

Web server: A computer on the Internet or intranet that serves as a storehouse for a Web page. When asked for a Web page by a browser, the Web server sends the page to the browser.

Web site: A collection of Web pages for an organization or an individual.

Webcast: Live audio and/or video telecast of events on the Internet.

whiteboard: A program that lets you view and edit a graphics image simultaneously with a remote Web user. ***See*** Part VI.

Wizard: A feature in Netscape Communicator that guides you through a particular process. For example, in Netscape Composer, you can use a Wizard to take a hand-held, guided tour of creating your own Web page.

World Wide Web: That part of the Internet which uses a combination of graphics, text, and multimedia.

Yahoo! (`www.yahoo.com`): A searchable database of information about and links to sites on the World Wide Web.

zipped file: A file which has been compressed using the PKZip or WinZip compression utilities. Often used to denote any compressed file, not just those created using PKZip or WinZip.

Index

Numbers

A

B

C

D

E

F

G

H

I

J

K

L

M

N

O

P

T

U

V

W

Y

Z

IDG BOOKS WORLDWIDE REGISTRATION CARD

Visit our Web site at http://www.idgbooks.com

IDG BOOKS WORLDWIDE
THE WORLD OF COMPUTER KNOWLEDGE®

ISBN Number: 0-76450-0414
Title of this book: Netscape Communicator™4 For Dummies®QR

My overall rating of this book: ❑ Very good [1] ❑ Good [2] ❑ Satisfactory [3] ❑ Fair [4] ❑ Poor [5]

How I first heard about this book:

❑ Found in bookstore; name: [6] ______

❑ Book review: [7] ______

❑ Advertisement: [8] ______

❑ Catalog: [9] ______

❑ Word of mouth; heard about book from friend, co-worker, etc.: [10]

❑ Other: [11] ______

What I liked most about this book: ______

What I would change, add, delete, etc., in future editions of this book: ______

Other comments: ______

Number of computer books I purchase in a year: ❑ 1 [12] ❑ 2-5 [13] ❑ 6-10 [14] ❑ More than 10 [15]

I would characterize my computer skills as: ❑ Beginner [16] ❑ Intermediate [17] ❑ Advanced [18] ❑ Professional [19]

I use ❑ DOS [20] ❑ Windows [21] ❑ OS/2 [22] ❑ Unix [23] ❑ Macintosh [24] ❑ Other: [25] ______ (please specify)

I would be interested in new books on the following subjects:

(please check all that apply, and use the spaces provided to identify specific software)

❑ Word processing: [26] ______ ❑ Spreadsheets: [27] ______

❑ Data bases: [28] ______ ❑ Desktop publishing: [29] ______

❑ File Utilities: [30] ______ ❑ Money management: [31] ______

❑ Networking: [32] ______ ❑ Programming languages: [33] ______

❑ Other: [34] ______

I use a PC at (please check all that apply): ❑ home [35] ❑ work [36] ❑ school [37] ❑ other: [38] ______

The disks I prefer to use are ❑ 5.25 [39] ❑ 3.5 [40] ❑ other: [41] ______

I have a CD ROM: ❑ yes [42] ❑ no [43]

I plan to buy or upgrade computer hardware this year: ❑ yes [44] ❑ no [45]

I plan to buy or upgrade computer software this year: ❑ yes [46] ❑ no [47]

Name: ______ Business title: [48] ______

Type of Business: [49] ______

Address (❑ home [50] ❑ work [51]/Company name: ______

Street/Suite# ______

City [52]/State [53]/Zip code [54]: ______ Country [55] ______

❑ **I liked this book!**

You may quote me by name in future IDG Books Worldwide promotional materials.

My daytime phone number is ______

❑ **YES!**

Please keep me informed about IDG Books Worldwide's World of Computer Knowledge. Send me your latest catalog.

...SECRETS®

3-D Visual

INFO WORLD TECHNICAL BOOKS

...FOR DUMMIES™ BESTSELLING BOOK SERIES FROM IDG

Macworld® Books

NO POSTAGE NECESSARY IF MAILED IN THE UNITED STATES

BUSINESS REPLY MAIL

FIRST CLASS MAIL PERMIT NO. 2605 FOSTER CITY, CALIFORNIA

IDG Books Worldwide
919 E Hillsdale Blvd, Ste 400
Foster City, CA 94404-9691